# Narratives of Muslim Womanhood and Women's Agency

Portrayals of Islamic teachings in mass media often present Muslim women as victims of patriarchal norms. Often covered in a full veil, and without individuality, they tend to be depicted using a monochrome image, across Muslim countries and regions. It does not portray the social reality and expectations of Muslim women, which are in fact diverse and contextual. This book consists of articles that attempt to answer the question, are Muslim women merely passive objects in constructing their role, despite the spread of social media and the Internet, the increased demands of earning disposable income for their families and their migration to non-Muslim countries around the world?

It closely examines women's agency in negotiating their role in Muslim-majority societies and in new places of settlement (Australia). These articles analyse Muslim women's narratives in a wide range of economic, political, social and cultural milieu and their relationship to identity construction and portrayal in the new millennium.

This book was originally published as a special issue of *Islam and Christian–Muslim Relations*.

**Minako Sakai** teaches at Indonesian Studies and Southeast Asian Social Inquiry School of Humanities and Social Sciences, at the University of New South Wales, Canberra, Australia. She has published widely on Islamic businesses, microfinance and women, development policies and identity politics in Indonesia. She is also an Adjunct Associate Professor at CAP, the Australian National University.

**Samina Yasmeen** is Director of the Centre for Muslim States and Societies and teaches Political Science and International Relations at the University of Western Australia. She has conducted extensive research on Islamisation, jihadism and women in Pakistan, as well as Muslim citizenship in Western liberal societies.

# Narratives of Muslim Womanhood and Women's Agency

*Edited by*
**Minako Sakai and Samina Yasmeen**

Routledge
Taylor & Francis Group

LONDON AND NEW YORK

First published 2018
by Routledge
2 Park Square, Milton Park, Abingdon, Oxon, OX14 4RN, UK

and by Routledge
711 Third Avenue, New York, NY 10017, USA

*Routledge is an imprint of the Taylor & Francis Group, an informa business*

*British Library Cataloguing in Publication Data*
A catalogue record for this book is available from the British Library

ISBN13: 978-1-138-56066-6

Typeset in Minion Pro
by diacriTech, Chennai

**Publisher's Note**
The publisher accepts responsibility for any inconsistencies that may have arisen during the conversion of this book from journal articles to book chapters, namely the possible inclusion of journal terminology.

**Disclaimer**
Every effort has been made to contact copyright holders for their permission to reprint material in this book. The publishers would be grateful to hear from any copyright holder who is not here acknowledged and will undertake to rectify any errors or omissions in future editions of this book.

# Contents

# Citation Information

The chapters in this book were originally published in two special issues of *Islam and Christian–Muslim Relations*. When citing this material, please use the original page numbering for each article, as follows:

**Introduction**
*Narratives of Muslim Womanhood and Women's Agency*
Minako Sakai and Samina Yasmeen
*Islam and Christian–Muslim Relations*, volume 27, issue 4 (2016) pp. 371–377

**Chapter 1**
*Performing Muslim Womanhood: Muslim Business Women Moderating Islamic Practices in Contemporary Indonesia*
Minako Sakai and Amelia Fauzia
*Islam and Christian–Muslim Relations*, volume 27, issue 3 (July 2016) pp. 229–249

**Chapter 2**
*Pakistan, Muslim Womanhood and Social Jihad: Narratives of Umm Abd Muneeb*
Samina Yasmeen
*Islam and Christian–Muslim Relations*, volume 27, issue 3 (July 2016) pp. 251–265

**Chapter 3**
*The Malaysian Islamization Phenomenon: The Underlying Dynamics and Their Impact on Muslim Women*
Bob Olivier
*Islam and Christian–Muslim Relations*, volume 27, issue 3 (July 2016) pp. 267–282

**Chapter 4**
*Negotiating Modernity: Women Workers, Islam and Urban Trajectory in Indonesia*
Nicolaas Warouw
*Islam and Christian–Muslim Relations*, volume 27, issue 3 (July 2016) pp. 283–302

**Chapter 5**
*Traditional, Islamic and National Law in the Experience of Indonesian Muslim Women*
Bernard Adeney-Risakotta
*Islam and Christian–Muslim Relations*, volume 27, issue 3 (July 2016) pp. 303–318

**Chapter 6**
*Between Texts and Contexts: Contemporary Muslim Gender Roles*
Shamim Samani
*Islam and Christian–Muslim Relations*, volume 27, issue 3 (July 2016) pp. 319–332

For any permission-related enquiries please visit:
http://www.tandfonline.com/page/help/permissions

# Notes on Contributors

**Bernard Adeney-Risakotta** is Professor of Religion and Social Science and Founding Director and International Representative at the Indonesian Consortium for Religious Studies in the Graduate School of Gadjah Mada University in Yogyakarta, Indonesia.

**Amelia Fauzia** is a Visiting Fellow at School of Humanities and Social Sciences, University of New South Wales Canberra, Australia. She is a lecturer at Syarif Hidayatullah State Islamic University Jakarta, Indonesia, and senior research fellow of the Religion and Globalisation Cluster at the Asia Research Institute, National University of Singapore.

**Bob Olivier** is based at the Centre for Muslim States and Societies, and Political Science and International Relations at the University of Western Australia.

**Minako Sakai** teaches at Indonesian Studies and Southeast Asian Social Inquiry School of Humanities and Social Sciences, at the University of New South Wales, Canberra, Australia. She has published widely on Islamic businesses, microfinance and women, development policies and identity politics in Indonesia.

**Shamim Samani** is Honorary Research Fellow at the Centre for Muslim States and Societies at the University of Western Australia.

**Nicolaas Warouw** is Lecturer in Indonesian Studies at School of Humanities and Social Sciences at the University of New South Wales, Australia.

**Samina Yasmeen** is Director of the Centre for Muslim States and Societies and teaches Political Science and International Relations at the University of Western Australia. She has conducted extensive research on Islamisation, jihadism and women in Pakistan, as well as Muslim citizenship in Western liberal societies.

# Narratives of Muslim Womanhood and Women's Agency

Minako Sakai and Samina Yasmeen

In Islamic teaching presented in the mass media, Muslim women tend to be portrayed as victims of patriarchal norms. Often covered in a full veil, and so without individuality, they tend to be depicted using a monochrome image across Muslim countries and regions. This is despite the fact that the social reality and expectations of Muslim women are diverse and contextual. Are Muslim women merely passive objects in constructing their role, despite the spread of social media and the Internet, the increased demands of earning disposable income for their families, and their migration to non-Muslim countries around the world?

This book, originally published in Volume 27.3 of *Islam and Christian–Muslim Relations*, a special issue entitled *Narratives of Muslim Womanhood and Women's Agency*, guest edited by Minako Sakai and Samina Yasmeen, and this introduction in Volume 27.4 of Islam and Christian-Muslim Relations, attempts to answer these questions. It closely examines women's agency in negotiating their role in Muslim-majority societies and in a new place of settlement (Australia). These chapters analyse Muslim women's narratives in a wide range of economic, political, social and cultural milieux and their relationship to identity construction and portrayal in the new millennium.

Narrative analysis has attracted attention since the publication of the seminal work by Scholes and Kellogg (1966), which clearly distinguished between empirical and fictional variants, and drew attention to the meanings inherent in oral or traditional narratives and the need to be mindful of these meanings. Subsequent progress in the field has resulted, among other trends, in the diversion of feminist analyses of narratives as ideo logical instruments from other analyses focused on narratives as purposive communi- cation (Scholes, Phelan, and Kellogg 2006). Others point to narratives being inherently political in their message and portrayal of identities. In an era of heightened focus on Islam's role in a globalized world and the identification of Muslim women as the signifier of difference, it becomes important to explore the extent to which Muslim women use or rely on narratives to portray their identities, and what this suggests about the diversity of experience, expectation and relationship to the socio-cultural and political milieux. Women's agency as an analytical point is of great importance because the traditional approaches to understanding Islam and gender have relied on textual interpretations of key Islamic sources, such as the Qur'an, often proffered by male scholars. Responding to this male dominance, female Muslim scholars have been gradually engaging with interpretations of the Qur'an and other key Islamic sources from a gender perspective (Barlas 2002; Mernissi 1987; Wadud 2006) and making way for the rise of so-called 'Islamic feminism'. Their contribution questions male agency in the delineation and construction of Muslim female identity. They have criticized the tendency to depict Muslim women as followers or victims of the process of instrumentalization of religion, which thereby reduces their agency in relation to Islamization. Furthering this work, the introductory section *Narratives of Muslim Womanhood and Women's Agency* highlights the agency of Muslim women in these processes.

This volume explores Muslim women's narratives in two innovative ways. The first is the acknowledgement of the importance of textual interpretation in Islamic studies, but with a shift of attention away from a philological approach towards an exploration of how specific socio-political contexts affect everyday experiences and legitimize particular social narratives and images of Muslim women. Socio-political contexts, in the scope of this work, include workforce demands deriving from economic development, international agendas put forward by international organizations, and the geographical location and nature of the state in which women live. As a particular result of the increasing need to maintain a consumer lifestyle in Muslim countries, unprecedented demands have been placed on women to manage their family's economic needs, whilst the rise of more conservative interpretations of Islam is tending to restrict their daily activities to the domestic sphere. These pressures are paralleled by a growing focus on women's agency in jihadist movements. While dramatically reflected in the recruitment drives targeting women by the so-called Islamic State (ISIS), the same phenomenon has also occurred in Palestine, Chechnya, Iran, Bosnia and Pakistan, to name but a few examples. Women have been engaged in oppositional discourses and militant activities with the express intention of avenging the mistreatment of male members of their families, or to defend the *umma* from the Western/non-Muslim onslaught. Consequently, for Muslim women, the struggle to negotiate their womanhood is not confined to the tasks of political activists pursuing the strengthening of women's rights in political or Islamic movements. Rather, as Osella and Soares (2010, 11) explain what they aptly call the 'islam mondain', ordinary Muslim women are negotiating their womanhood in everyday life and in politics, including in both the secular and Islamic spheres. Examining the development of this theoretical approach to understanding Muslim life, the special issue presents case studies of narratives of Muslim womanhood from Asia and Australia. We have included countries with significant Muslim populations and influence such as Pakistan, Indonesia and Malaysia, and also Australia as an example of a new place of settlement for migrant Muslim women that does not have a Muslim-majority population.

The second innovative approach is to examine the emergent Islamic authorities deriving from Muslim women. Chapters in this edited volume examine how the emergence of new Islamic authority, coupled with state policy, education and the availability of media and penetrating liberal Western values, is affecting or promoting particular images of Muslim womanhood, and how it shapes Muslim women's narratives about themselves and their environment. New religious transformations through the use of media and technology are not limited to Muslim societies in Asia, but can also be found in Africa (Eickelman and Anderson 2003; Hackett and Soares 2015). To illustrate the popularity of media and technology among Muslims, Indonesia, a newly democratized country which has the largest Muslim population in the world, has the largest number of Facebook users. With the decline of Islamic schools as the main education provider (Hefner 2008), Indonesian Muslims are now expanding their Islamic knowledge actively through school textbooks and Internet resources rather than seeking it from local Islamic scholars (Sakai and Fauzia 2014). Islamic preachers frequently appear on television programmes where they provide practical ideas about how to manage family life. Islamic knowledge has also fused with modern management training and is used in business training sessions in Indonesia (Howell 2013; Rudnycky 2010). The consequence of this increased popularity of the practical application of Islamic knowledge to business development for women is that females regularly conduct Islamic study groups and engage in charitable and business activities. As a result, Islamic study groups that were once confined to members of associations that had connections with mainstream Muslim women's groups (Van Doorn-Harder 2006) are now rapidly expanding, and groups are forming from neighbourhoods, workplaces and social groups. Furthermore, as it reflects the decline of traditional Islamic authorities in Indonesia (Fealy and Bush 2014; Feener 2014; Sakai 2012), this situation calls for a scholarly enquiry into Muslim women's agency in promoting narratives. With a focus on Indonesia, Blackburn, Smith, and Syamsiyatun (2008) and Rinaldo (2013) have published seminal works on Muslim women's efforts to negotiate their identities by focusing on Muslim women in leadership positions. The chapters in this edited book or volume broaden the range of Muslim women under study and explore a wider geographical context.

The scope of the enquiries in this book includes emergent challenges in Muslim women's lives, such as the work–family balance, and support for jihad arising from the challenges of modernity and political and strategic instability in, for example, the Middle East and South Asia. Research indicates that, while a gap exists between educational and employment opportunities available to women, who constitute half of the 1.6 billion Muslims in the world, the speed with which women have progressed in these fields is phenomenal. It has been aptly described as 'compress[ing] into a few short years the half-century evolution from Betty Friedan's *The Feminine Mystique* to Sheryl Sandberg's *Lean In*' (Zahidi 2015). Zahidi has drawn attention to the fact that, in Turkey, women's enrolment in universities increased proportionately from 75% of the rate for men in 2005 to 85% in 2015. In Egypt, the number of women enrolled in universities nearly equals the number of men. In the Gulf countries, the rate of female enrolment in tertiary institutions is three times higher than that for men. A similar situation exists in Saudi Arabia, where the number of women in these institutions continues to increase. These rapid shifts also impact on women's access to the labour market. Though traditional role specifications have by no means disappeared, a greater number of women are participating in the labour market in general. The proportion of women in professional positions has also increased in countries such as Pakistan. Zahidi (2015) estimates that '[n]early 40 million Muslim women have joined the labor force in the past ten years: among them, 9 million in the Arab world, 8 million in Indonesia, 7 million in Pakistan, 7 million in Bangladesh, 2 million in Turkey, and 1 million in Malaysia'. This is not to suggest that women's access to education and labour markets has translated into 'inclusive growth' where benefits extend equally to men and women in both the economic and political spheres. Research indicates, however, that there is increasing female representation at higher levels of decision making (Sperling, Marcati, and Rennie 2014). While this is occurring, some women are being enticed by ISIS's recruitment drive: in Pakistan, for example, one woman reportedly left with her four children to join the 'jihad' in Syria, and the Pakistani government has arrested approximately 40 women on suspicion of intending to join ISIS (AFP 2015; NDTV 2016). Malay-Indonesian women are not immune from the enticement to support jihad either, as Rahmah (2016) shows.

This volume comprises six chapters deriving from case studies highlighting the negotiation and narratives of Islamic womanhood in Asia and Australia. Five articles highlight the impact of pressing social expectations on Muslim women in Indonesia, Malaysia and Pakistan, and Samani's article explores Muslim womanhood in Australia, as an example of a place of settlement for migrant Muslim women.

The first chapter, by Minako Sakai and Amelia Fauzia,'Performing Muslim Womanhood: Muslim Business Women Moderating Islamic Practices in Contemporary Indonesia', examines how Muslim women – particularly educated middle-class women with strong Islamic commitments – juggle domestic responsibilities and professional career paths. The recent Islamization process in Indonesia has various causes, but one is the spread of education, with religion a compulsory school subject. The Indonesian government has provided resources to increase access to education and the number of Muslim university graduates has consequently increased. This emergent group of Muslim graduates need to combine their professional aspirations with the conservative Islamic gender roles found in their everyday life. For them, an Islamic microfinancing institution offers an attractive workplace that enables them to combine their career aspirations and their Islamic values. Sakai and Fauzia highlight the importance of creative interpretations of Islam provided by working women who provide narratives of appropriate Islamic womanhood to avoid social stigma. Their case presents a middle way of negotiating their Muslim womanhood in the social and economic context of contemporary Indonesia.

The second chapter, 'Pakistan, Muslim Womanhood and Social Jihad: Narratives of Umm Abd Muneeb', by Samina Yasmeen, turns our attention to another emergent social issue in the Muslim world: jihad. It is important to understand the ways in which women participate in and support jihad in order to assess the impact of Islamization in Muslim societies, particularly in Pakistan, where jihadist organizations perpetrate attacks on a regular basis. Yasmeen argues that, against the backdrop of growing militancy in Pakistan, Islamist groups have relied on female agency to propagate ideas of Muslim womanhood that encompass the family and societal spheres. She sheds light on how their interpretations of Muslim womanhood are employed to support the jihad project in the family environment, as well as its transcendence across the family–society divide. This article shows that female narratives by women that specifically address female audiences, using culturally specific language, allow for the possibility of modifying audience frames of reference and may prepare them to support what could be broadly conceived of as the jihad project.

Robert Henry Olivier's chapter, 'The Malaysian Islamization Phenomenon: The Underlying Dynamics and Their Impact on Muslim Women', takes us to Malaysia, where, over the last few decades, the state has strongly supported Islamization as part of its nation-building. The establishment of Islamic courts and a religious police force has accelerated the process of institutionalization of Islam in Malaysia. Muslim divorces are dealt with in the Sharia court. Drawing on qualitative data to explore the views of professional Malay women, Olivier contends that professional Muslim Malay women's concerns about the trajectory of Islamization in Malaysia reflect their expectations that their rights and mobility may be further curtailed should the current patterns of Islamization in Malaysia continue. However, the existing socio-political context discourages them from voicing their concerns in public.

Nicolaas Warouw's chapter, 'Negotiating Modernity: Women Workers, Islam and Urban Trajectory in Indonesia', sheds light on the impact of urbanization and industrialization in Indonesia. Since the early 1970s, the Indonesian government has made efforts to attract foreign investment in the manufacturing sector. With this change, young women started to find new employment opportunities in urban factories in Indonesia, migrating there from the country side. Warouw examines how young Muslim working-class women negotiate their modernity through their experience in Islamic study groups. Islam here serves to mediate between the two worlds these women simultaneously belong to: their urbanized working lives and the world of the Islamic values they developed while growing up in rural areas.

Bernard Adeney-Risakotta's chapter, 'Traditional, Islamic and National Law in the Experience of Indonesian Muslim Women', provides an analysis of the legal frameworks Muslim women in Indonesia face in comparison with those in Pakistan. He points out that, in Indonesia, a woman's role is framed not only by national law, but also by Islamic law and customary law known as adat. What women are entitled to as an inheritance is determined by the negotiations of legal pluralism surrounding women's rights. Adeney-Risakotta shows that patriarchal values in Islamic laws are rather normative, not necessarily restricting a Muslim woman's presence in the public sphere in Indonesia, because legal pluralism enables diverse social ideas of womanhood, including the liberal notion that men and women are equal.

Shamim Samani's chapter, 'Between Texts and Contexts: Contemporary Muslim Gender Roles', is focused on the interpretations of gender roles for Muslim migrants in a new place of settlement, namely, Australia. Australia offers a liberal Western setting that challenges the patriarchal gender norms of migrant Muslim families. Samani's research shows that traditional Muslim gender roles are being affected by economic imperatives and the liberal gender equality notions found in Australia, but the degree of its impact is mediated by the influence of the cultures of the countries of origin of the Muslims.

The initial idea for this book was derived from a workshop entitled 'Narratives of Muslim Womanhood: Contemporary Analysis', held in December 2013. The workshop was part of on-going research collaborations on the issue of Muslim womanhood between Dr Minako Sakai, the chair the Asia Pacific Seminar Series at School of Humanities and Social Sciences, at the University of New South Wales, Canberra, and Professor Samina Yasmeen, the Director the Centre for Muslim Societies and States at the University of Western Australia. We thank both institutions for funding the workshop and for all their support. We have benefited from the advice from the journal editors and reviewers of *Islam and Christian–Muslim Relations* in the editing process, and thank them for their assistance.

## A way forward

The chapters in this book show that Muslim women are consciously taking control of the production of appropriate gender roles by constructing their own narratives. The case studies, which come from four countries and incorporate professional and working-class women, highlight that women's agency provides a key to understanding the social realities of Muslim womanhood.

As a way of concluding this overview of the special issue, we suggest future research directions.

First, the ways in which women seek their Islamic knowledge are becoming increasingly diverse in the digital age. Women are actively participating in female-only on-line discussions on Islam (Piela 2013), whilst the popularity of female preachers emerging on television programmes involving live participants in women's Islamic study groups is growing. Muslim women are under increasing pressure to generate an income as a result of economic necessity and to manage their household while balancing work and family life, and this is a crucial area for future research. Empirical studies on Islamic authorities among Muslim women and the medium of Islamic knowledge transmission would highlight the future of social ideas and trajectories of the narratives of Muslim womanhood.

Second, a need exists to explore women's narratives of access to education and employment, as well as the way they experience inclusive environments as Muslim minorities in Western liberal states. Though data exists on the lack of such access and the problems encountered, it would be beneficial to hear women's voices and discover how they link their narrative to the need for active intervention by Muslim communities and the governments of their respective states. Finally, research into narratives of women's participation in jihad needs further exploration. Instead of restricting research to the current focus on female recruitment by ISIS, a need exists to broaden the scope of investigation to assess the narratives employed by males and females affiliated with jihadist organizations to promote female activism in the jihad project, and the spaces demarcated for this activism. Such detailed investigation would contribute to the broader agenda of constructing counter-narratives aimed at preventing the radicalization of women.

The study of women's narratives, it is essential to note, remains an interdisciplinary project and one that requires greater attention to the stories and voices of women themselves. The ultimate benefit to human society would be in the form of greater female agentic contributions to societal development, as well as the development of strategies to counter negative narratives.

## Disclosure statement

No potential conflict of interest was reported by the authors.

## References

AFP. 2015. "Pakistan Police Uncover Women-led ISIS Fundraising Network: Official." *AFP*, December 21. Accessed June 26, 2016. http://english.alarabiya.net/en/News/asia/2015/12/21/Pakistan-police-uncover-women-led-ISIS-fundraising-network-official.html.

Barlas, Asma. 2002. *Believing Women in Islam: Unreading Patriarchal Interpretations of the Qur'an.* Austin: University of Texas Press.

Blackburn, Susan, Bianca J. Smith, and Siti Syamsiyatun. 2008. *Indonesian Islam in a New Frontier: How Women Negotiate Their Muslim Identities.* Clayton: Monash University Press.

Eickelman, Dale, and Jon Anderson. 2003. *New Media in the Muslim World: The Emerging Public Sphere.* Bloomington: Indiana University Press.

Fealy, Greg, and Robin Bush. 2014. "The Political Decline of Traditional *Ulama* in Indonesia." *Asian Journal of Social Science* 42 (3–4): 536–560.

Feener, R. Michael. 2014. "Muslim Religious Authority in Modern Asia." *Asian Journal of Social Science* 42: 501–516.

Hackett, Rosalind I. J., and Benjamin Soares. 2015. *New Media and Religious Transformations in Africa*. Bloomington: Indiana University Press.

Hefner, Robert W. 2008. "Islamic Schools, Social Movements, and Democracy in Indonesia." In *Making Modern Muslims: The Politics of Islamic Education in Southeast Asia*, edited by Robert W. Hefner, 55–105. Honolulu: University of Hawaii Press.

Howell, Julia D. 2013. "'Calling' and 'Training'." *Journal of Contemporary Religion* 28 (3): 401–419.

Mernissi, Fatima. 1987. *Beyond the Veil: Male–Female Dynamics in a Muslim Society*. Bloomington: Indiana University Press.

NDTV. 2016. "100 Pakistanis Left for Syria, Iraq to Join ISIS." *World Press Trust of India*, January 5. Accessed January 26, 2016. http://www.ndtv.com/world-news/100-pakistanis-left-for-syria-iraq-to-join-isis-1262380.

Osella, Filippo, and Benjamin Soares, eds. 2010. *Islam, Politics, Anthropology*. Oxford: Wiley-Blackwell.

Piela, Anna. 2013. "'Women are Believers in Their Own Right': One Muslim Woman's Challenge to Dominant Discourses Shaping Gender Relations in Islam." *The Muslim World* 103: 389–403.

Rahmah, Unaesa. 2016. "The Role of Women of the Islamic State in the Dynamics of Terrorism in Indonesia." *Middle East Institute*, May 10. Accessed June 30, 2016. http://www.mei.edu/content/map/role-women-islamic-state-dynamics-terrorism-indonesia.

Rinaldo, Rachel. 2013. *Mobilizing Piety: Islam and Feminism in Indonesia*. Oxford: Oxford University Press.

Rudnycky, Daromir. 2010. *Spiritual Economies: Islam, Globalization, and the Afterlife of Development*. New York: Cornell University Press.

Sakai, Minako. 2012. "Preaching to Muslim Youth in Indonesia: The *Dakwah* Activities of Habiburrahman El Shirazy." *Review of Indonesian and Malaysian Affairs* 46 (1): 9–32.

Sakai, Minako, and Amelia Fauzia. 2014. "Islamic Orientations in Contemporary Indonesia: Islamism on the Rise?" *Asian Ethnicity* 15 (1): 41–61.

Scholes, Robert, and Robert Kellogg. 1966. *The Nature of Narrative*. Oxford: Oxford University Press.

Scholes, Robert, James Phelan, and Robert Kellogg. 2006. *The Nature of Narrative: Fortieth Anniversary Edition*. New York: Oxford University Press.

Sperling, J., C. Marcati, and M. Rennie. 2014. *GCC Women in Leadership – from the First to the Norm*. McKinsey. Accessed June 30, 2016. http://www.mckinsey.com/global-locations/europe-and-middleeast/middle-east/en/gcc-women-in-leadership.

Van Doorn-Harder, Pieternella. 2006. *Women Shaping Islam: Reading the Qur'an in Indonesia*. Chicago: University of Illinois Press.

Wadud, Amina. 2006. *Inside the Gender Jihad: Women's Reform in Islam*. Oxford: Oneworld.

Zahidi, S. 2015. "Women in the Muslim World Taking the Fast Track to Change." *Women Matter Series*. Accessed June 30, 2016. http://www.mckinsey.com/industries/social-sector/our-insights/women-in-the-muslim-world-taking-the-fast-track-to-change.

# Performing Muslim Womanhood: Muslim Business Women Moderating Islamic Practices in Contemporary Indonesia

Minako Sakai and Amelia Fauzia

**ABSTRACT**

Islam is increasing its influence in contemporary Indonesia. What impact does this have on women's economic activity? In Indonesia there is a strong expectation that women should work. Working outside of the home, however, frequently poses a challenge for Muslim women, especially wives. The growing influence of Islamist (women's) groups in Indonesia strengthens conservative Islamic values to some extent. Nevertheless, a growing number of Muslim women in Indonesia are working to earn an income to meet their household's needs. As traditional Islamic teaching prescribes that men should be the main breadwinners for their family, and Indonesian Family Law (1974) also stipulates that husbands are the head of the household, economically successful married women have been put into an awkward position. In view of this development, this article explores how Indonesian middle-class Muslim women have been negotiating between their Islamic values and economic necessity. The article shows that the need to generate an income has led to working Muslim women moderating their Islamic values, enabling them to justify extending their responsibilities into the public domain. We argue that working Muslim women are playing a key role in moderating Islamic theological interpretations and perceptions of Islamic womanhood in contemporary Indonesia.

Question: 'Have you ever attended an Islamic study gathering where the preacher has suggested that women should stay at home?'

Answer: 'Never.' 'If he did, he would immediately be challenged (*didemo*).' 'We would not attend such meetings!' (Focus group discussion with Muslim women)

## Introduction

After the fall of Suharto's centralist government in 1998, the democratization of Indonesia has proceeded remarkably well. Indonesia is now a thriving lower-middle-income country, and a relatively stable democracy in Southeast Asia. The growing middle class, with its strong desire for consumption and better education for its children, has led to a more expensive standard of living and there is therefore a growing demand for households to have two incomes to cope with their financial needs (Utomo 2012, 66–68). Younger, lower-middle-class women are also drawn into paid work because they want to have consumer-based urban lifestyles (Naafs 2012, 54).

An interesting challenge for Indonesia is that over 85% of its population are Muslims, giving it the largest Muslim population in the world. Islam and expressions of Islamic faith have been important parts of the identity of the emergent middle class (Fealy and White 2008). Political parties with a strong Islamist orientation influenced by Islamist ideas from the Middle East, such as the Prosperous Justice Party (Partai Keadilan Sejahtera – PKS), represent the lower sections of the pious middle class in Indonesia (Rinaldo 2010). The PKS was once popular and well supported, but its popularity has more recently declined, as reflected in the results of recent Indonesian elections (2009 and 2014). Its decline in popularity has been due – among other things – to cases of corruption and the behaviour of party leaders. Such Islamist groups tend to uphold the view that a women's main role is based on the biological aspect of their gender, and that domestic responsibilities, particularly relating to taking care of the family, belong to women. For example, PKS women point to the Qur'an to support the claim that these gender roles are natural and, on the basis of this interpretation, their view of gender equality lies in sharing moral equity between men and women rather than achieving social equality (Rinaldo 2013, 136).[1]

It is worth noting that, apart from these Islamist women, a growing number of Muslims in Indonesia are also showing support for Islamic causes and Islamic orientations, even though their support for Islamist political parties has stalled (Sakai and Fauzia 2014). Middle-class Muslims are predominantly educated in secular schools and contact with the two mainstream Islamic organizations in Indonesia, Nahdlatul Ulama (NU) and the Muhammadiyah,[2] declines and becomes intermittent as Muslims reach adulthood. However, their middle-class identity is indicated by their consumption of a wide range of Muslim products, such as Muslim clothing (Beta 2014), halal food, and Muslim travel needs (Fealy 2008).[3] More importantly, they are generally committed to implementing Islamic teaching, actively use the Internet and social media (Hosen 2008) and turn to popular culture for Islamic knowledge as they make a conscious effort to become better Muslims in their everyday life (Weintraub 2011).

As a result, the increasing need for money to support a consumer-based lifestyle, coupled with their desire to be good Muslims, has put pressure on women to generate an income to meet these needs. Recent research findings (Bahramitash 2002; Blackburn 2008; Rinaldo 2008; Robinson 2008) show that Islamism has not always confined Muslim women solely to the domestic sphere in Indonesia. However, they have been placed under pressure to justify their Muslim womanhood if they engage in paid employment because of the long-standing Islamic assumption that domestic responsibilities constitute women's natural role in society. Their situation is further complicated as male-dominated Islamic authorities in Indonesia, such as the Indonesia Council of Ulama (Majlis Ulama Indonesia – MUI), tend to promote conservative Islamic teachings to discourage women's participation in paid work, as we shall outline below.

Only upper-middle-class women with stable financial resources may have the option of staying at home and being ideal Muslim women, taking care of their families without having to manage that role along with paid work. In contrast, lower-middle-class Muslim women need to work to meet their lives' financial demands, and women's participation in the workforce in Indonesia increased from 32% in 1971 to 52% in 2002 (Utomo 2012, 65). Historically, many women have worked in informal sectors to generate an income to meet their own and their family's financial needs, but the pressure to generate an income has increased in recent years. For example, according to a recent report (Asia Foundation 2013, 10), small and medium enterprises (SMEs) in Indonesia generate 56% of Indonesian GDP and employ more than 96% of the workforce. Women are an important segment of the workforce and are also employers, as about 30% of SMEs are owned by women. In some cases, as we highlight in this article, Muslim women are becoming stable income earners in urban areas.

In the light of this development, this article will examine how married Muslim female entrepreneurs in Indonesia are negotiating their Muslim womanhood by juggling work and domestic responsibilities.[4] We shall focus on married middle-class Muslim women who are closely affiliated with the circle of *Baitul Maal wat Tamwil* (BMT). BMTs are emergent Islamic Savings and Credit cooperatives that also undertake Islamic charitable activities. We shall examine the profiles of Muslim women who are married and work to support their family. The BMTs offer financial services to SMEs, which are often owned by women. BMTs themselves are also predominantly classified as SMEs. As their business schemes are regulated by Islamic jurisprudence, BMTs tend to merge professional development programmes with Islamic values in managing businesses (Antonio 2008) and to employ only Muslims. Thus, the employees are predominantly Muslims who are committed to Islamic causes, while their clients are SMEs. We show that these middle-class working Muslim women endeavour to define their interpretations of Muslim womanhood to endorse and justify their contested role as income-generator and family carer. We argue that, while these Muslim women have not squarely challenged conservative Islamic gender roles, they have been disseminating non-radical non-Islamist teaching, which enables them to actively participate in paid work in Indonesia. Married and working, these women are mediating the practice of Islam against the spread of Islamist ideas of domesticated womanhood, which are increasingly permeating the public sphere in contemporary Indonesia. We argue that working Muslim women are creating an appropriate and acceptable alternative Islamic womanhood, which runs counter to the narrowly defined role of Muslim women as domesticated and subordinated, without turning to international feminist movements for support. In contemporary Indonesia, Islamic authorities have become very diffuse and individual Muslims have more autonomy in locating diverse religious interpretations (Feener 2014; Sakai 2012). Reflecting this development, we argue that working middle-class women have informed themselves of Islamic tenets by recourse to a wide range of sources; they sometimes perform their acceptable submissive gender role to defend their family from criticism, but tacitly practise an alternative Islamic womanhood that enables them to pursue paid work and entrepreneurship to generate an income to cater for their family's financial needs.

The structure of the article is as follows. First, we present the change in women's employment opportunities in Indonesia. We show that women are increasingly moving into the service and informal sectors of the Indonesian economy, including SMEs, to generate an income. Second, we analyse national and Islamic discourses on womanhood in contemporary Indonesia. This section explains how ideas of contemporary Indonesian citizenship and Islamic womanhood have merged. The third section analyses how middle-class married women juggle and balance their role by reinterpreting Islamic teaching and performing expected Muslim gender roles to avoid criticism of their activities. We argue that married working middle-class women justify their role in paid work with reference to Islamic teaching and cultural norms, but tacitly promote their version of Islamic woman-hood, which is compatible with the modern demands of work and family.[5]

## Women's participation in the waged workforce in Indonesia

Indonesia has successfully developed its economy since the 1970s, and the country's changing economic landscape has affected employment and also increased women's workforce participation. Between 1987 and 2002, the Indonesian economy grew strongly, despite the setbacks of financial crises, averaging 7% per year in that period (Suryadarma, Suryahadi, and Sumarto 2012, 554) and Indonesia has achieved the status of a lower-middle-income power since the 1990s (Rhee 2012). Gradual industrialization and urbanization have played a key role in reducing agriculture as a main economic activity, although it still accounted for 16% of economic output in 2009, which is larger than countries of similar development levels (Reserve Bank of Australia 2011, 35). On the other hand, the positive economic growth rate has enabled the government to increase funding for education and Indonesian school enrolment has increased, although there is some inequality; data suggest slightly more male students than females tend to finish their nine-year basic education (BPS 2011, 30–31). With by the rapid expansion of industrialization, the contribution of agriculture to the country's GDP declined from 53% in the mid-1960s to less than 20% in the 1990s, while the contribution of industry and manufacturing grew to over 60% of GDP in the 1990s (Brown 2012, 736–737) and continued to grow in the 2000s. Along with this change, commercial services and manufacturing/mining have become an important source of employment, as has the public sector (Parker and Ford 2008). In 2009, manufacturing accounted for 12% of total employment (World Bank 2012, 4).

The impact of support for education and the availability of job opportunities in urban areas have encouraged women to pursue tertiary and professional education for employment. For example, the percentage of women in the labour force increased from 27% in 1960 to 41% in 2000 (Utomo 2012, 65). Furthermore, women have been choosing to study business and accounting at the tertiary level since the mid-1990s. In 2004, more than half of the tertiary students studying business and accounting were female (Lindawati and Smark 2010, 33). It is worth noting that female participation in the workforce has also been assisted by Indonesia's successful family planning programme, which began in the 1970s. The fertility rate was 6.0 in 1970 but fell to 2.59 by 2000 (Bennett 2012), which means that women limit their child-bearing years and have greater possibilities for find productive work. Furthermore, women's participation in the workforce received international policy endorsement because of the gender mainstreaming programme officially endorsed by the United Nations' Conference on Women in Beijing in 1995. Since 2000, the Indonesian government has been following the Beijing Platform and has introduced policies to support gender mainstreaming programmes and achieve gender equality, including Presidential Instruction No. 09, 2000 on gender mainstreaming. This instruction highlights that all development programmes need to have a balanced gender involvement.

Despite the implementation of new policies, the availability of job opportunities and professional education training, and the widespread expectation that families will become smaller in size, Indonesian women have not been tempted to participate in paid work to their full capacity. Indonesian females seldom advance to managerial positions (Lindawati and Smark 2010, 33). Executive and senior managerial positions are perceived as being more suitable for men (World Bank 2011, 207). Furthermore, Indonesian women do not actively seek higher managerial positions since the government promotes the idea of husbands being the head of households and wives as being housewives through the Marriage Law of 1974 and the nation-wide Family Welfare Program (Pendidikan Kesejahteraan Keluarga/Family Welfare Education or PKK).[6] As housewives, women are responsible for everything related to domestic household matters, such as cooking and taking care of children, and they leave responsibility for working in the hands of husbands. This stipulation indirectly justifies the pressure that women feel not to pursue paid work or a career but rather to be mothers and housewives. Consequently, they are generally happy to remain secondary to their husbands in generating income for the family (Utomo 2012).

Another important finding is that SMEs provide a livelihood for over 90% of the country's workforce, especially for women and young people (Tambunan 2007, 33). However, the rate of the ownership of SMEs by women in Indonesia lags behind that in other East Asian countries (Asia Foundation 2013, 10), even though Indonesian women play the main role in developing SMEs. Nevertheless, economic necessity does push women to seek new sources of income. For example, overseas migrant work is an emergent area in which low-skilled women are actively seeking employment as domestic servants in Saudi Arabia, Malaysia, Singapore and Hong Kong. Migrant work has been promoted by government agencies since the 1990s and the number of women employed in this way has gradually increased. There are currently an estimated 6.5 million Indonesian overseas workers, of whom 75–80% are domestic workers (Saifuddin 2014). When these women are single, they send regular remittances to their families in Indonesia, and they end up spending longer working as domestic servants in order to maintain this income (Anggraeni 2010). Furthermore, many women continue to work overseas even after they have a family of their own, as finding an alternative source of income at home to support their family is not easy. Sri Lanka, the Philippines and Indonesia are all countries that send large numbers of workers abroad, and more than half of these legal migrant workers are employed in unskilled domestic work, and the majority of them are married women with at least one child (Ukwatta 2010). They leave home to earn an income so they can send remittances to provide for a quality education for their children.

In view of these recent changes in Asia, suffice it to say that women in Indonesia face a predicament if they give paid work priority over their family, due to factors such as 'state *ibuism*' (a state definition of women's main role as being in the domestic realm, from *ibu*, Indonesian 'mother'), especially if they are Muslim women, as will be further explained below:

First, the Suharto government's New Order promoted the understanding of appropriate womanhood as being reflected in their duty to take care of the family. As mentioned earlier, women are expected to become wives and mothers and this idea is promoted by the PKK national programme. At the same time, the wives of male public servants become members of a state-run women's organization called Dharma Wanita

(Women's Duty), in which a woman's position is determined by her husband's place in the hierarchy. Dharma Wanita is led by wives of government officials, who occupy leadership roles because of their husbands' positions. These women run the Family Education Program. The word *ibu*, meaning 'mother' in Indonesian, is commonly used in Indonesia to refer to an adult woman, suggesting that all women are mothers. According to Surya-kusuma (1996, 101), 'state Ibuism defines women as appendages and companions to their husbands, as procreators of the nation, as mothers and educators of children, as house-keepers, and the members of Indonesian society – in that order.' Being a housewife reflects the domestic role that the state has been promoting, and it is also a status symbol associated with being a middle-class Indonesian family (Bennett 2012). Working outside the home in paid work, neglecting the responsibilities of being a mother and a wife, challenges not only expectations of marital relations but also the state's expectations of womanhood. Indonesia's democratization since 1998 has weakened 'state *ibuism*' because the state now encourages women to participate widely in public life,[7] but, despite this change, engagement in paid work outside the home remains a challenge for middle-class women, including Muslim women.

Second, Muslim women are facing further challenges from Islamic values. Traditional Islamic authorities perceive women's natural place to be in the home. Traditional Islamic values position women as mothers and wives, not as breadwinners. Such views are strongly justified by referencing Hadith (traditions of the Prophet) and *fiqh* (Islamic law), including speeches made by Islamic scholars. This is especially the case in rural areas. Despite the persistence of Islamic conservatism, there have been some changes, however. For example, women's gender movements have recently arisen from within Muslim communities based on re-interpretations of women's rights as they are portrayed in Islamic sources.[8] Furthermore, since the 2000s, female Islamic preachers, such as Mamah Dedeh, have been promoting moderate views on the role of women in public through television (TV) presentations. Popular TV programmes are also giving time to both male and female *da'i* (preachers) in the hope that this novelty will attract viewers.

This strong sense that women's main responsibility is in the domestic realm can be found in various Islamic edicts (*fatwas*) issued by the MUI. Although Islamic edicts in Indonesia are not legally binding and can be ignored, they are seen as an important source of Islamic judgement in contemporary Indonesia. For example, the MUI issued a *fatwa* that prohibits women from working as migrant workers abroad (*tenaga kerja Indonesia* – TKI) if there is no male companion or other guarantee that their honour will be protected. The MUI *fatwa* No. 7/2000 stipulates that a woman's priority is to take care of her family. By-laws in some regions, such as in the Aceh province and Tan-gerang District of West Java, have prohibited women from going out at night and require women to ask permission from their husbands to work outside the home or even simply to go somewhere. However, this did not prevent the wave of TKI going abroad increasing from year to year (Schapendonk 2012). The lack of suitable opportunities in Indonesia and lucrative earning opportunities open to the female workforce overseas have indirectly led to Muslim women disregarding such *fatwas*. The spread of new media and mass education has led to sources of Islamic authority becoming fragmented and diversified, particularly among educated middle-class Muslims (Sakai 2012),[9] while many lower-middle-class women have to work due to economic necessity. We have observed that lower-middle-class working women rarely buy Islamic books to seek information because books are expensive and hard to read. Instead, they tend to rely on Islamic interpretations provided by local community members and TV, and in these mediums the traditional view of the role of Islamic women still has a strong presence.

The third factor is the result of globalization and modernization, which have brought a wave of Middle Eastern Islamism, a new form of Salafism and Islamic values, to Indonesia (Azra 2002). These new Islamist ideas have affected the perception of Islamic womanhood, especially among middle-class Muslims, by highlighting women's domestic responsibilities. Rinaldo (2008) finds that Islamist organizations and political parties, such as Hizbut Tahrir Indonesia and the PKS, have created a habitus for middle-class Muslim women that provides a certain level of modernization and which does not prohibit women from working, but still resonates with their traditional gender values. 'Women may have careers as long as they prioritise domestic work' (Rinaldo 2008, 33). In order to achieve this, working Muslim women employ a strategy, namely, wearing headscarves (*jilbab*) in public. By wearing *jilbab*, they publicly show that they are prioritizing piety, including the commitment to act appropriately in a woman's role (Mernissi 2003). Although this type of Islamic womanhood has not been unanimously agreed upon, we argue that the arrival of Islamist ideas from the Middle East has further strengthened the Islamic theological interpretations that a present woman's role as primarily domestic.[10]

## Methodology

Taking into consideration the theological and economic challenges facing working Muslim women in Indonesia, we shall now examine how Muslim womanhood has been negotiated and promoted, particularly among the growing BMT and the SME sectors in Indonesia, where lower-middle-class women predominate in the workforce. Muslim women's reconstruction of their womanhood has not been entirely compatible with traditional and emerging Islamist interpretations, or with the long-running state campaign of motherhood.

Noting that commercial services in urban areas are among the growing sources of employment in Indonesia, and that women have been playing the dominant role in developing SMEs, we have focused on female entrepreneurs associated with the Islamic financing institutions known as BMTs. Indonesia started providing modern Islamic financial services in the early 1990s with the establishment of the first Islamic bank, Muamalat Bank (Hefner 1996). Islamic micro-finance is a financial service targeting SMEs in urban areas and it developed as a grass-roots financial institution in Indonesia supported by Muslim activists. BMTs offer financial services, such as savings and credit services, based on Islamic jurisprudence and have been growing in the urban areas of Indonesia since the early 1990s. BMT founders and employees are exclusively Muslims who have a strong motivation to work for social justice by offering inclusive financial services by starting a BMT or working for BMTs. Administratively, the BMT sector has been separate from the banking sector and has been growing rapidly in urban areas of Indonesia to support the SMEs (Antonio 2008).

Through our research on the development of BMTs, we have collected data, including published material, on profiles of female BMT workers, executives and BMT clients, who are predominantly SME traders (Muttaqin et al. 2011). Since 2008, we have spoken with more than 25 female managers, clients and founders of BMTs in Jakarta, Central Java, West Java, East Java, South Kalimantan and South Sulawesi. Our meetings with informants took the form of focus group discussions and open-ended interviews. Out of the range of informants, we have chosen to profile three Muslim women in this article, as they are perceived as role models among working Muslim women in the BMT and SME sectors because of their ability to run their businesses as well as fulfilling their Muslim womanhood responsibilities towards their families. For example, BMT Beringharjo has collected profiles of their female clients and BMT workers including the two women, Rambe and Indri, and published them in a booklet (Muttaqin et al. 2011) to inspire middle-class business women and their clients. They hold leadership positions in Islamic study groups and Islamic charitable and business activities and are often seen as mentors for other Muslim women. We therefore consider that their fulfilment of Muslim womanhood is representative of the ideal contemporary Muslim woman held in esteem in the SME sector. Three case studies also show existing women's general Islamic affinity with mainstream organizations (the Muhammadiyah and NU), but they are not the only Islamic sources these women turn to. Other diffused Islamic authorities have arisen in contemporary Indonesia for Muslim women to consult. In the following section, we shall explore the narratives of these Muslim women to examine how they interpret Islamic teachings to validate their own circumstances.

## Profiles of SME Muslim women entrepreneurs

### High-profile BMT managers

#### Mursida Rambe

Mursida Rambe was born in Medan, North Sumatra in 1967. Her father was a trader and her mother was a housewife. Her family lived on a modest income. Her parents regarded education as very important and passed that value on to her. She finished her junior high school education at an Indonesian government-approved Islamic high school in Medan and then moved to Yogyakarta. She went to a senior high school affiliated with Muhammadiyah in Yogyakarta and then continued her university education at the University of Muhammadiyah, where she majored in *dakwah*, Islamic propagation and communication. She started Islamic propagation as a member of Corps Dakwah Pedesaan (CDP or Village Corps) in an impoverished area of the District of Gunung Kidul, in Yogyakarta Special Province. The CDP was led by an Islamic preacher who was able to attract supporters of both the NU and Muhammadiyah in Yogyakarta due to the inclusive nature of the teaching that was given. Rambe tried to propagate Islam, explaining to the community how to be a good Muslim according to Islamic teaching, but she realized that impoverished people could not concentrate on Islamic teaching because they had to focus much more on how to survive and on obtaining enough food. After 10 years of trying to propagate Islam, she did not think there was a significant change in the community and came to the realization that poverty had to be relieved if she wanted her Islamic propagation to succeed. She wondered what measures she could take within the guidelines of Islamic jurisprudence. That was around 1994, when the Dompet Dhuafa (DD) Foundation[11] was starting to circulate the idea of an Islamic economy for social justice. Her brother brought her an advertisement in the newly established Islamic daily, *Republika*, for a training opportunity at a BMT. She was selected for the training together with two other CDP activists. After her training and apprenticeship in a rural bank, she raised 1 million rupiah with her friends and received a further 1 million from the DD to start a BMT near the Beringharjo market in the centre of Yogyakarta. The small traders often borrowed money from illegal money lenders who charged high rates of interest, and defaulting on small loans could result in small traders losing property or possessions. Having grown up in Medan of North Sumatra, near a traditional market, she had seen how cruel these illegal money lenders and the high interest rates could be and felt that social justice required that alternative financial services should be provided. The BMT consists of both for-profit and not-for-profit wings in order to offer inclusive financial services that comply with Islamic teaching (Sakai 2008, 2014). This was the beginning of BMT Beringharjo, which now has 12 branches in Java and more than 100 employees. In 2014, its assets were estimated to be worth 50 billion rupiah.[12]

BMT Beringharjo has an active *baitul maal*, a not-for-profit social wing, offering a variety of creative schemes to reduce poverty in the community. For-profit businesses also have an innovative investment scheme to encourage long-term investment from Indonesian migrant workers in Hong Kong, which have been used as seed funding to start a new BMT in the region, where poverty was rife and access to credit was difficult. The goal of this saving scheme is to encourage migrant workers to save a substantial amount of money so that they could use the capital for future businesses back in Indonesia, and their investment is also being actively used in a poor region where access to credit was limited. Mursida Rambe is not only the director of BMT Beringharjo but also the secretary of important Islamic economic organizations in Indonesia.

Even though Rambe attended Muhammadiyah educational institutions, she no longer retains any official relations with the Muhammadiyah. She was one of the BMT founders and has maintained close relations with the DD, which does not have a particular Islamic orientation but is an organization founded by Muslims who have been through the state system of education. What she sees as important is the concept of *dakwah bil hal*, or propagation by action, a method used by preachers such as Ahmad Dahlan, the founder of Muhammadiyah. As a result of her unfruitful experience in propagation activities and their limitations, Rambe thinks it is important to take concrete action. Like the DD, her company makes Islamic study group meetings part of its training. The BMT regularly invites Islamic scholars who can interpret the meaning of Islamic texts or qur'anic verses to speak to workers at the organization. She has frequently been invited to provide guidance on work ethics to BMT cooperatives through the Indonesian regional government, and on these occasions she also preaches the importance of social justice and encourages Islamic almsgiving (*sedekah* and *zakat*). She regularly addresses the female traders' Islamic study group at the mosque next to the Beringharjo market and also connects with Indonesian women's Islamic study groups inside and outside Yogyakarta to conduct charitable activities to help the poor and disadvantaged through her *baitul maal*.

*Islamic womanhood.* After starting her BMT in 1998, Rambe married a Javanese man, Umar Jumirin, and they have three children. She gives credit to her husband for her business success, as he is always supportive and is a source of inspiration. According to Tickamyer and Kusujiarti (2012), this is common behaviour for husbands of women who work outside their homes, so that they are not stigmatized for being bad wives and mothers. Despite her demanding work life, Rambe says she gives priority to her family as a wife and a mother. If she is at home, she tries to focus on her family and not be disturbed by her work. In reality, she often travels interstate and overseas and is not always able to get home before her children go to bed. In Indonesia, particularly among the middle-class families, domestic duties such as cooking, child-minding, shopping and cleaning are commonly performed by maids. Thus, the actual task of cooking for her family is not considered to be one of her highest priorities as a mother. Rather, caring for her children and her husband is her core duty. For example, when Rambe goes away, she often talks to her children on the phone and wishes them good night, and she also makes sure that she does not stay away from her family if it is possible to go home. She said it was important to receive permission (*izin*) from her husband, but it was more appropriate to say that she informed her husband and sought his moral support rather than asking him for formal permission.

Rambe's personal assistant is a female employee and she works closely with her; she tries to avoid situations where she is left alone with a male colleague or business partner if this is feasible. She received a Kartini Award from a well-established Indonesian women's magazine in 2011 for being an inspirational female entrepreneur. Rambe's husband runs a small business, but as the director of the BMT she earns more than her husband. She does not believe that women who work outside the home are going against Islamic teaching, as Islam encourages Muslims to do good work for their community. If there are opportunities, and if a person has the capacity to do good for the community, they should work (*amal*) for the benefit of society and she believes that the more good work Muslims undertake, the more likely they are to enter Heaven. Rambe believes that the BMT has provided her with ample opportunities to work for the common good. When asked if she would stop working if her husband did not approve of it, she said she would, if his argument was valid and it prohibited her from working. But her husband laughed this off saying that she would not be happy at home if she did not have anything else to do, so she should continue leading the BMT. Her husband shared her view that, if she is useful to society and there is demand for her work, she should continue to do good for the community. Indeed, Rambe's work and businesses has provided an important source of family income and raised the status of the family.

### Hamidah

Hamidah is a 40-year old female entrepreneur from Martapura, a small jewellery town in South Kalimantan, who is married with four children. Her family was involved in the NU but she went to public schools (rather than Islamic schools) from primary school to university (she attended Lambung Mangkurat University). She is the manager of two BMTs in Martapura (one of which had assets worth Rp. 14 billion in 2013), and she owns a small real estate company and a childcare business. After graduating from university, majoring in economics, she was invited by Kyai Jazuli, a local leading NU Islamic scholar, to become the manager of the BMT Khoirul Ikhwan and Khoirul Amin (the two BMTs that he had established), which are affiliated with a *pesantren* (Islamic boarding school) and the local NU. To date, she has successfully managed these two BMTs. In her spare time, especially early in the morning, she watches NU-operated *ahlusunnah wal jamaah* TV (an Islamic channel launched in 2013), which promotes traditional NU values, and she listens to Islamic sermons given by Islamic popular preachers, such as Arifin Ilham and Quraish

Shihab. She also reads a wide range of religious books, such as books on Abdul Qadir Jailani, an important figure for traditionalist Muslims, and on the family life of the Prophet.

Living in a strongly Islamic environment, she sees her position as that of a Muslim woman, a mother, and a business person. Her income is much higher than her husband's, and so is her social status. He helps Hamidah by assisting with printing activities related to her BMTs. She said that being a business person is not a problem at all as long as her husband grants her permission to do this work. He supports her work and allows her to travel without him. She said that work is permissible as long as it does not disturb her domestic tasks as mother and wife. She recalled that once her husband did not allow her to start a new business which was located far from home. She followed her husband's advice and cancelled her plans. This is the only time that her husband did not give her permission to follow her business enterprises, and she thinks his advice was appropriate. She told us that, as long as women are honest with and respect their husbands, it is not difficult to get permission from their husbands to developing businesses.

*Islamic womanhood.* Hamidah is aware that there are qur'anic verses and teachings that are interpreted to mean that it is better for women to stay at home. Responding to these, she argued that the context in Indonesia is different from that of the Middle East, and it is difficult to implement these strict teachings in Indonesia:

> Yes, I heard a lot about that, even though we are not an Islamic law expert. In fact it is true that women in Saudi Arabia do like that. However, for women like us, who are living in Indonesia, it is difficult to only stay at home, considering our daily expenses [we have] to meet. We are working to help our husband[s]. We should work to reduce our family's economic burden. If we wanted to go for *umrah* or *hajj* [together],[13] of course we need money to travel. If I have a lot of successful businesses, I could automatically also contribute a lot to our dream. And this is better [than just waiting]. (Interview with Hamidah)

She has indeed been on an *umrah* with her husband, funded by her own business's profit.

She does not see any problem in interpreting things differently from certain Islamic teachings. She said:

> I know that some people talked about that in religious gatherings. I heard about that myself. We saw in the markets of Makkah and Madinah in Saudi Arabia, almost all of the merchants were men. No female merchants were visible. But, we know that their living quality is good and their social welfare is assured. I think if we did that in our country, it would be difficult.

As the situation in Indonesia, especially with regard to economic and social conditions, is different from Saudi Arabia, Hamidah maintains that in the Indonesian context women can work to improve the family's living conditions. She argues that even Islamic scholars have different opinions relating to women's economic participation and Muslims may follow their own choice of Islamic preachers. She said:

> ulama, guru or kyai [Islamic scholars] sometimes differ in their opinions ... the most important thing for me is [that] I have a religious scholar whom I could turn to for their opinion. In Martapura we have KH Jazuli Usman (called Guru Seman), a well-known religious scholar here.

Hamidah said Guru Seman is a modern scholar and has moderate views. She even used to ask various questions and consult with a *kyai* she knew very well about her problems. Visiting a learned religious scholar (*alim*) is better than visiting a rich person. When this *kyai* passed away, she began to consult with Guru Nouval, another charismatic *kyai* in Martapura. However, her sources of Islamic knowledge are not limited to local Islamic authorities or NU circles. She also regularly tries to obtain Islamic knowledge by watching TV programmes and reading Islamic books, so that she consults a wide variety of Islamic teachings.

Responding to a question about the fact that some women, including herself, earn more than their husbands, who are traditionally regarded as the head of family and have responsibility for providing financially for the family, Hamidah said that the *rejeki* (fortune) could come from either the husband or the wife. In her case, *kyai* Jazuli advised her and her husband that if in their case the *rejeki* came through the wife, that was acceptable. It did not matter through whom *rejeki* came to the family. The most important thing was how the husband and wife managed it. Hamidah had been conducting business before her marriage, which meant that she frequently had to go out. Now, although she has a lot of work outside the house, she only goes out once she has finished her domestic duties.

Although Hamidah strongly argues for the importance of wives working, she does not agree that women should become community leaders, including head of state, quoting Q 4.34: *al-rijālu qawwāmūna ʿalā al-nisāʾ* (men are stronger than women). It is better for women not to become leaders if there are suitable men for the role, but they can help male leaders.[14] For example, a woman should not become president, but she could become a minister. So Hamidah does not feel comfortable about being the chair of a BMT board (*pengurus*), but is happy to serve as a director of BMTs because she was trusted to serve where no suitable male candidate was available. However, she maintains that if there is no choice, women could become leaders, and they should be accepted because this is *amanah* (being entrusted by a community to take responsibility for completing important tasks). Hamidah likens community leaders to political leaders, so she does not agree with women becoming community leaders, which is a view shared widely among NU affiliates and members. In addition, interestingly, she does not think of herself as the permanent leader of the BMTs. She believes that she has taken up a leadership role because there is no eligible man who could function in her position. She sees this as being in line with Islamic jurisprudence, and that this is considered to be an emergency, and temporary, situation (*darurat*).

Hamidah is accustomed to holding regular meetings for the staff from two of her BMTs. Even though she calls them gatherings or meetings and not Islamic study groups (*pengajian*), she always invites a *kyai* or *guru* to talk on a topic such as Islamic law, to give religious advice and even to comment on the strategic planning of BMTs. Hamidah sees her role as being a Muslim woman with an important responsibility to her community. She is proud to say that she wakes up early in the morning to cook for the whole family and washed clothes every night when she comes home from her daily work. By juggling her business activities and her domestic tasks, she feels that she is fulfilling her role as a Muslim woman well. For her, womanhood is not only about being a good wife and mother, but also about contributing to the family's income and giving back to society. This double burden is indeed very heavy for women, but with their strong belief in

Islamic gender roles, they do not see it as a burden; rather, these are the duties they need to perform in order to become good Muslim women.

In the next section we shall turn our attention to a successful SME business woman who has developed her business in partnership with BMT Beringharjo.

### Endah Susetyo Indriyati (Indri)

Indri grew her business from a small amount of initial capital and gradually developed it to its current successful state; she owns three grocery shops, a car rental service, and restaurant/cafe businesses in Yogyakarta. She was born in Banjarnegara in 1972. Her father was a teacher who also ran a small shop. She received a secular education and, when she was in junior high school, her father had an accident and was no longer able to work. Her mother took over the running of the shop, but Indri had to assist by working in it. She finished public high school and obtained a two-year college degree (Diploma 2) majoring in secretarial studies. She worked for a company, PT Swadaya Upaya, which enabled her to live on the outskirts of Yogyakarta for a time. She thought her fate, and even her children's future, would be better if she moved to Yogyakarta, which is the centre of higher education and a vibrant city with many tourists. She then took up another position in a company and married her husband, Hamid, in 1994. To prove that her business had expanded from a very small shop, in 2008, at the initial stages of our meetings, she showed me a photo of when she started her shop and had just given birth to her twin boys. Her photo showed her in very plain clothing and she told me that her economic situation was very limited as her husband's salary was small. She borrowed Rp. 200,000 (equivalent to USD 93 at the time) from Hamid's parents and started a clothing sales business while nursing her young children. She knocked on neighbours' door for sales. In order to develop her business, she kept book-keeping and accounting records and made sure that her business was profitable. After gaining some business experience, in 1998 she borrowed Rp. 3 million (equivalent to USD 333 at the time) from her parents-in-law and started her first shop, Kembar Satu (No.1 Twins). Her shop stocks basic food, drinking water and also gas cylinders commonly used for cooking in Indonesia. Her clients became loyal, as her service was very friendly and personal, and the customers found the prices competitive. She thinks business successes come through broadening her business relations. Thus she has always been diligent in expanding her networks and seeks business opportunities and sponsorships for social events.

*Islamic womanhood.* Indri's husband became ill in 2002, not long after she opened the first shop. Since then, he has suffered from a series of illnesses and since 2008 he has been resting at home, and she has been the family breadwinner. She has faced a variety of challenges, including her husband's and sons' illnesses, but she has still built up her businesses successfully. She sees herself as a woman who is good at business, and she sees no problem with supporting her family. For her, the most important thing is to give her Islamic duties priority over undertaking business. She has made the *hajj* (obligatory pilgrimage) with her husband and has undertaken *umrah* (voluntary pilgrimage) every two years, when it was possible to do so. The money spent could have been used to further her business, but she believes that undertaking Islamic duties is important, and that everything she has is a loan from God (*titipan dari Allah*). She makes sure she performs the Islamic ritual prayers as required, and she also attends a variety of Islamic study groups for women. In 2013, she started a restaurant and café business that trades in the evening and she decided to invite her neighbours to use it for the study of Islam during the day, when the building is empty. She pays for the preachers and provides the venue free of charge as she sees this activity as an act of religious devotion (*amal*), and considers it important to give and to do good for the community as a Muslim. She remembers how hard life was for her after her father became ill, and she has fostered disadvantaged children (as many as four), believing that everything belongs to God, not to herself. She has survived a variety of challenges, particularly her husband's illnesses, but she believes that God helps her. She does as much community service and Islamic voluntary giving (*sedekah*) as she can to assist the disadvantaged through Islamic study groups and her charitable networks.

In addition to God's help, Indri believes that her business success is due to her husband, who has trusted her and allowed her to develop her entrepreneurial talent. She thinks her businesses are very creative and also enable her to do good. While pursuing her business career, she completed a university degree and then a Master's degree in business management and was given an award for her outstanding academic performance. She is not ashamed of being a breadwinner and a woman married to a stay-at-home husband and she always introduces her husband to her new friends and business contacts. Her business meetings and networks take her away from home, including interstate business trips. Her business success has led to her being appointed to serve on various social councils, such as school councils and as a volunteer. In an interview, she said that this was not a problem, as it is a professional requirement and proof that she has been recognized as a useful member of the community. What is important is that her husband endorses all her business and social activities. She is fulfilling the duties Islam asks of Muslims and she is delighted to have opportunities to do so.

### Muslim womanhood: negotiating Islam and everyday economic rationality

The above profiles of three Muslim women actively involved in small business development all show the following features:

1. The success of their businesses is highly commended, even though they are women. The first wife of the Prophet Muhammad was a successful businesswoman and her example is well remembered and used as a reference point for aspiring Muslim businesswomen. For example, her name is commonly used for Muslim women's groups. Although none of the informants mentioned her specifically as their role model, Muslims find it difficult to negate the financial contributions made by the Prophet's first wife to her husband, and thus, her example reminds them of this precedent of female entrepreneurship.
2. These women feel uneasy with the long-standing Islamic perception that a woman's main duty is to be a family carer. However, they have not directly challenged Islamic authorities such as the NU or Muhammadiyah to initiate theological debates on Muslim womanhood. Rather, they have expanded their Islamic knowledge through mass media and Islamic study groups, and advocated that Muslim womanhood is compatible with business success as long as their husband agrees to and supports their work. They also share such views through their business networks to promote their Islamic womanhood. They all give credit to their husbands for

supporting them and contributing to their ability to succeed. All three women clearly mention their husband's role, and the importance of receiving permission from them in their role as working women. Our findings concur with observations of Javanese women, as analysed by Tickamyer and Kusujiarti (2012). With the presence of strong cultural and Islamic views that women should be primarily family carers, women in the BMT circle try to play down their public role to honour their husbands as the head of the family, in line with state norms and conservative ideas of Islamic womanhood.

3. These women strongly argue that their business activities are beneficial not only to their families but also to their communities. They highlight the Islamic teaching that doing good works (*amal*) for the community is their duty as Muslims. They are not trying to construct a particular perception of womanhood, but rather promoting what Muslims are expected to do, as long as they do not neglect their primary duty to care for their family. Rambe and Indri are also instrumental in running Islamic study groups for women, where they disseminate the importance of Islamic almsgiving and care for the community while pursuing business and profit.

4. As Hamida has shown, these women advocate that Muslim women, if they have been entrusted with something (*amanah*), are expected to deliver on their commitment to become leaders, irrespective of their gender. This view promotes independence and self-reliance for women, without depending on men for running their businesses. However, these women are still sometimes uncomfortable with the public perception that they are leaders. They try to downplay their achievements by saying that they are undertaking normal activities.

Thus, these women are embodying and promoting an emergent Islamic womanhood, whose traits are not gender-specific. In other words, they are advocating a counter representation of Islamic womanhood that is not bound to the domestic sphere alone. Rather, their Islamic womanhood combines their long-standing primary duty as wife and mother with their Islamic duty to work for the common good and for the betterment of their society. As a result, even though none of them mentioned international feminism or a gender mainstreaming agenda, or challenged Islamic theology, they are in fact creating an appropriate and acceptable alternative Islamic womanhood that is counter to the narrowly defined role of a domesticated and subordinated traditional Muslim woman.

The above narratives also clearly show that these women use the traditional keyword 'permission' to leave their homes and that they receive support from their husbands and families, as well as from their communities, to undertake their entrepreneurial activities. In order to receive permission, these women have juggled their work and family lives rather than neglecting or abandoning their domestic duties. If women fulfil their role as mothers and wives, they are likely to be allowed to undertake activities outside home. The 'permission' is instrumental within the *fiqh* discussion. For example, the MUI *fatwa* on overseas migrant workers states that women may go abroad to work if they have their husband's permission. These Muslim women endeavour to follow Islamic teachings, but they are quite proactive in choosing which Islamic authorities they consult and seek religious advice that is likely to endorse and justify their combined role as an income-generator, family carer and wife. The quotation at the very beginning of this article, referring to women protesting against Islamic preachers who encourage women to stay at home, is a reflection of their critical approach to religious advice or what is regarded as Islamic teaching.

It is important to note, however, that, for most women affiliated with BMTs, the permission they seek from their husbands is not so much permission in a formal sense, but simply agreement. Because of the strong need for income to meet the family's financial requirements, most husbands encourage their wives to find paid work even outside the home. In reality, some women work for BMTs far away from their husbands and children. For example, a middle manager of the BMT Amanah Muamalat in Kendari, in Southeast Sulawesi, stated in a group discussion that she stays and works in Kendari, her husband works in another city, and their daughter stays with her mother on the Island of Java. But, importantly, this living arrangement had to be agreed to by her husband.

Asking for permission should be interpreted as a religious and cultural strategy to defend both husbands and wives against conservative views of gender roles. It preserves the husband's position as the head of the family and locates wives in a position of submission to their husbands, as conservative Muslims have long expected. Thus, what working Muslim women and their husbands have demonstrated is what Butler (1990) has called 'gender performativity', by which she means that the notion of gender is built on a sequence of acts and expressions.

In contrast to Rinaldo's (2006, 2008) interpretation of Islamic womanhood, as found among Islamist groups, Islamic womanhood in the BMTs reflects the strong economic needs, either of the women's families or of their communities. Working Muslim women endeavour to show *fikih bil hal*, or *fiqh* in practice. They interpret certain Islamic teachings in a way that moderates Islamic practices in Indonesia, where conservative Islamic ideas are dominant. They conform to the existing notion of Islam in their actions while also displaying an alternative Muslim womanhood compatible with the reality, which demands that women be economically successful.

Islamic teachings and practices have been transformed and adapted according to the place and time in which Muslim women have found themselves. Within institutions with strong Islamic values and teachings, they interpret Muslim womanhood through their positions as advocates of Islamic micro-finance and as career women, as well as in their positions as role models in their local communities. What these women have done is transform Islamic practices so that they are relevant to their own context. Although they know that some teachings say that women should stay at home, husbands are the head of the family and the obligation to provide an income or fortune (*rejeki*) rests with the husband, they have justified their positions in various ways: by arguing for the family's need for income generation, by justifying their actions as contributing to the Islamic community, and by seeking support from certain relevant religious authorities.

Women in BMT circles generally, not only in the case of Hamidah outlined above, seek advice from Islamic scholars who support their economic activities and the benefits of their networks. Almost all the women we interviewed during a focus group discussion (December 2013) mentioned that they followed a moderate *kyai* such as Mamah Dedeh, Maulana, Yusuf Mansur, including specific figures from Ikatan Cendekiawan Muslim Indonesia (Indonesian Muslim Intellectual Association), who established BMTs. In addition to these national Islamic preachers, these women have developed regular communication with Islamic scholars, whom they consult on many things, including their difficulties as entrepreneurs and their status as women.

The reason why these Muslim women entrepreneurs do not really adhere to gender-specific roles presumably relates to the discourse of wealth, which does not differentiate between men and women. Even though, within *fiqh* discourse, men, or husbands, are regarded as the head of the family and as responsible for earning income, the flexibility of *fiqh* means that it may easily change. Hamidah's explanation set out above lends credibility to her argument about welfare. A BMT staff member even asked why, in a difficult situation, women or wives would not want to help their husbands earn a living. Thus, juggling work and family care is not regarded as a burden by these women; it is a challenge they have to face in modern times. In fact, their female entrepreneurship is moderating Islamic practice in everyday life and protecting them from irrelevant Islamic values developed from a distinct Middle Eastern *fiqh* context that is very different from the environment found in Indonesia.

## Conclusion

This article has analysed how middle-class businesswomen have succeeded in realizing an Islamic womanhood that combines the conflicting tasks of being a family carer and a business woman. The current Indonesian situation requires middle-class Muslims to generate an income that will support their lifestyle, which requires additional financial resources. In order to justify combining their diverse roles, Muslim women acknowledge the importance of men's position as the head of the household, and seek permission from their husbands to continue their work. Their gender performativity enables them to counter potential criticisms based on conservative Islamic and cultural gender norms. However, and importantly, our case studies have shown that middle-class working Muslim women, particularly those working closely with the BMT and small business sectors, are tacitly promoting an alternative Islamic womanhood by juggling their work and family. We argue that these working Muslim women, without substantially challenging Islamic theology, are playing a key role in moderating Islamic theological interpretations and perceptions of Islamic womanhood in contemporary Indonesia. They negotiate their *fiqh* by selecting interpretations of Islam that are relevant to their local context thanks to the diffusion of Islamic authorities and the availability of diverse sources of Islamic teaching. These women are creating a strategy of using Islamic microfinance institutions to play an important role in mediating the practice of Islam and working against the spread of conservative Islamist ideas of womanhood and the influx of rigid Islamist ideas that are permeating the public sphere in contemporary Indonesia.

The findings of this article further concur with important recent studies (Arnez 2010; Beta 2014; Blackburn, Smith, and Syamsiyatun 2008; van Doorn-Harder 2006; Robinson 2008; Rinaldo 2006, 2008, 2013) highlighting diverse ideas of Islamic womanhood in contemporary Indonesia. We emphasize that there is a need for further research to examine a broader spectrum of Islamic authorities, and their creation, which underpin contemporary Islamic womanhood. There is also a need to explore how a variety of ideas of womanhood have created a milieu in which Muslim women may validate their own ideas of Islamic womanhood that are appropriate for their context.

## Notes

1. However, political participation of Traditionalist Islamist women is higher than women from moderate Islamic groups. See Blackburn (2008).
2. The NU (www.nu.or.id) and Muhammadiyah (www.muhammadiyah.or.id) are the biggest Islamic organizations in Indonesia and were created during the colonial period. The NU is regarded as a Traditionalist Muslim organization that strictly follows the four schools of Islamic law, but it tends to be accommodating towards other religious traditions. Its following is strong in rural areas. The Muhammadiyah is regarded as a Modernist Muslim organization that seeks to purify religious practice from local traditions and develop it with more rational and modern religiosity. Its following is strong in urban areas. Both the NU and the Muhammadiyah hold generally moderate views of Islam.
3. The growing middle class in Indonesia is also represented by groups (*hijabers*) of young women who wear fashionable long Muslim veils, called *hijab*.
4. This article will use standard Indonesian forms of Islamic expressions.
5. However, we do not intend to argue that Islamic womanhood is limited to working women. We accept that young women's employment opportunities are limited in Indonesia and marriage provides a pretext for educated unemployment (Naafs 2012).
6. This programme was introduced into the school curriculum for PKK in 1957. It is no surprise that the notion that a woman's role is to be a housewife is strong, since this curriculum has been nationally implemented in all public schools beginning at primary school level. The PKK abbreviation was applied to the Pembinaan Kesejahteraan Keluarga (Family Welfare Programme), which was no longer only a subject taught in schools but also a movement supported by government offices from the village to the national level. In the Reformation period the name of the PKK was changed to Pemberdayaan dan Kesejahteraan Keluarga (Family Welfare Empowerment), to highlight the advocacy of this movement or programme.
7. The government has a target of having 30% of the House of Representatives members being women.
8. Studies criticizing the conservative understanding of women's roles have increased with the presence of female Islamic NGOs, such as Rahima (Hidayah 2012).
9. Muslims may look beyond the MUI or Indonesian Islamic organizations to seek alternative fatwas, religious guidance, and *fiqh* opinions from anyone, including Internet sources known jokingly as kyai Google (*kyai* is a title given to an Islamic scholar) (Hosen 2008). New types of religious authorities may provide women with an opportunity to opening up new interpretations and even challenge traditional ideas, such as views on polygamous marriages and the possibility for women to seek a career. Online discussions and forums are becoming an important source of negotiation for various views on gender relations (Piela 2010).
10. Rinaldo (2006) finds that different types of organizations, such as the liberal Rahima and the conservative PKS, have created distinct conceptions of Islamic womanhood based on their different understandings of Islam and gender.
11. The DD (www.dompetdhuafa.org) is a community-based Islamic charity in Indonesia, established in Jakarta in July 1993 by young journalists from an Islamic newspaper called *Republika*, Erie Sudewo and Parni Hadi. *Dompet* means 'wallet' and *dhuafa* means 'the poor', so the name means a wallet for the poor. *Republika* itself is part of the movement of Indonesian Muslim intellectuals called Ikatan Cendekiawan Muslim Indonesia (Indonesian Muslim Intellectual Association), and is a part of the political Islam of the New Order regime. The DD is among the leading Islamic charitable organizations undertaking Islamic philanthropic programmes in Indonesia.
12. Website: http://www.bmtberingharjo.com/pages-99-About%20Us.html (accessed October 7, 2014).
13. Islamic devotional activities such as voluntary or obligatory pilgrimages (*umrah* and *hajj*) cost USD 3219 per person in 2014 in Indonesia.

14. A similar argument was used by Islamic groups, including the NU, to disapprove of Megawati Sukarnoputri becoming the first female president of Indonesia in 1999. See Robinson (2008) for details.

## Disclosure statement

No potential conflict of interest was reported by the authors.

## Funding

We acknowledge funding support from the University of New South Wales Canberra to enable an Asia Pacific Seminar Series titled Narratives of Muslim Womanhood: Contemporary Analysis, co-hosted with the Centre for Muslim States and Societies, the University of Western Australia and held at UNSW Canberra in December 2013.

## References

Anggraeni, D. 2010. *Dreamseekers: Indonesian Women as Domestic Workers in Asia*. Jakarta: Equinox.

Antonio, M. S. 2008. "Islamic Microfinance Initiatives to Enhance Small and Medium-Sized Enterprises." In *Expressing Islam: Religious Life and Politics in Indonesia*, edited by G. Fealy and S. White, 251–266. Singapore: ISEAS.

Arnez, M. 2010. "Empowering Women through Islam: Fatayat NU between Tradition and Change." *Journal of Islamic Studies* 21 (1): 59–88.

Asia Foundation. 2013. *Access to Trade and Growth of Women's SMEs in APEC Developing Economies: Evaluating the Business Environment in Indonesia*. Jakarta: Asia Foundation.

Azra, Azyumardi. 2002. "Globalization of Indonesian Muslim Discourse: Contemporary Religio-Intellectual Connections between Indonesia and the Middle East." In *Islam in the Era of Globalization: Muslim Attitudes towards Modernity and Identity*, edited by J. Meuleman, 31–50. London: Routledge.

Bahramitash, R. 2002. "Islamic Fundamentalism and Women's Employment in Indonesia." *International Journal of Politics, Culture, and Society* 16 (2): 255–272.

Bennett, L. R. 2012. "Infertility, Womanhood and Motherhood in Contemporary Indonesia: Understanding Gender Discrimination in the Realm of Biomedical Fertility Care." *Intersections: Gender and Sexuality in Asia and the Pacific* 28. Accessed September 29, 2015. http://intersections.anu.edu.au/issue28/bennett.htm.

Beta, A. R. 2014. "Hijabers: How Young Urban Muslim Women Redefine Themselves in Indonesia." *International Communication Gazette* 76 (4–5): 377–389.

Blackburn, S. 2008. "Indonesian Women and Political Islam." *Journal of Southeast Asian Studies* 39 (1): 83–105.

Blackburn, S., B. J. Smith, and S. Syamsiyatun. 2008. *Indonesian Islam in a New Era: How Women Negotiate Their Muslim Identities*. Clayton, VIC: Monash University Press.

BPs (Badan Pusat Statistik). 2011. *Statistik Gender 2011*. Jakarta: Badan Pusat Statistik.

Brown, G. K. 2012. "Trade, Employment and Horizontal Inequalities in New Order Indonesia." *European Journal of Development Research* 24 (5): 735–752.

Butler, J. 1990. *Gender Trouble: Feminism and the Subversion of Identity*. New York: Routledge.

van Doorn-Harder, P. (2006). *Women Shaping Islam: Reading the Qur'an in Indonesia*. Urbana: University of Illinois Press.

Fealy, G. 2008. "Consuming Islam: Commodified Religion and Aspirational Pietism in Contemporary Indonesia." In *Expressing Islam: Religious Life and Politics in Indonesia*, edited by G. Fealy and S. White, 15–39. Singapore: ISEAS.

Fealy, G., and S. White. 2008. *Expressing Islam: Religious Life and Politics in Indonesia*. Singapore: ISEAS.

Feener, M. R. 2014. "Muslim Religious Authority in Modern Asia: Established Patterns and Evolving Profiles." *Asian Journal of Social Science* 42 (5): 501–516.

Hefner, R. W. 1996. "Islamizing Capitalism: On the Founding of Indonesia's First Islamic Bank." In *Toward a New Paradigm: Recent Developments in Indonesian Islamic Thought*, edited by M. R. Woodward, 291–322. Tempe: Arizona State University.

Hidayah, Nur. 2012. "Feminising Islam in Contemporary Indonesia: The Role of Progressive Muslim Women's Organizations." PhD diss., University of Melbourne.

Hosen, N. 2008. "Online Fatwa in Indonesia: From Fatwa Shopping to Googling a Kiai." In *Expressing Islam: Religious Life and Politics in Indonesia*, edited by G. Fealy and S. White, 159–173. Singapore: ISEAS.

Lindawati, A., and C. J. Smark. 2010. "Education into Employment? Indonesian Women and Moving from Business Education into Professional Participation. (Report)." *e-Journal of Business Education and Scholarship Teaching* 4 (2): 29–42.

Mernissi, Fatima. 2003. "The Meaning of Spatial Boundaries." In *Feminist Postcolonial Theory: A Reader*, edited by Reina Lewis and Sara Mills, 489–501. New York: Routledge.

Muttaqin, A., R. M. Amtsar, Nuri Mashril, and A. Pratiwi. 2011. *Perempuan yang Menginspirasi: Kisah Sukses Mitra BMT Beringharjo*. Yogyakarta: BMT Beringharjo and Dompet Dhuafa.

Naafs, S. 2012. "Navigating School to Work Transitions in an Indonesian Industrial Town: Young Women in Cilegon." *The Asia Pacific Journal of Anthropology* 13 (1): 49–63.

Parker, L., and M. Ford. 2008. *Women and Work in Indonesia*. London: Routledge.

Piela, A. 2010. "Muslim Women's Online Discussions of Gender Relations in Islam." *Journal of Muslim Minority Affairs* 30 (3): 425–435.

Reserve Bank of Australia. 2011. *Bulletin*. Sydney: Reserve Bank of Australia.

Rhee, Changyong. 2012. "Indonesia Risks Falling into the Middle-Income Trap." *Jakarta Globe*, March 27.

Rinaldo, R. 2006. "Contesting Womanhood in Two Indonesian Islamic Organizations." *Antropologi Indonesia* 30 (1): 21–35.

Rinaldo, R. 2008. "Muslim Women, Middle Class Habitus, and Modernity in Indonesia." *Contemporary Islam* 2 (1): 23–39.

Rinaldo, R. 2010. "The Islamic Revival and Women's Political Subjectivity in Indonesia." *Women's Studies International Forum* 33 (4): 422–431.

Rinaldo, R. 2013. *Mobilizing Piety: Islam and Feminism in Indonesia*. New York: Oxford University Press.

Robinson, K. 2008. *Gender, Islam and Democracy in Indonesia*. Hoboken, NJ: Taylor and Francis.

Saifuddin, Irham Ali. 2014. "A Promise to Domestic Workers, after 10 years." *Jakarta Post*, March 18.

Sakai, M. 2008. "Community Development through Islamic Microfinance: Serving the Financial Needs of the Poor in a Viable Way." In *Expressing Islam: Religious Life and Politics in Indonesia*, edited by G. Fealy and S. White, 267–286. Singapore: ISEAS.

Sakai, M. 2012. "Preaching to Muslim Youth in Indonesia: The Dakwah Activities of Habiburrahman El Shirazy." *Review of Indonesian and Malaysian Affairs* 46 (1): 9–31.

Sakai, M. 2014. "Establishing Social Justice through Financial Inclusivity: Islamic Propagation by Islamic Savings and Credit Cooperatives in Indonesia." *TRaNS: Trans-Regional and –National Studies of Southeast Asia* 2 (2): 201–222.

Sakai, M., and A. Fauzia. 2014. "Islamic Orientations in Contemporary Indonesia: Islamism on the Rise?" *Asian Ethnicity* 15 (1): 41–61.

Schapendonk, J. 2012. "Confined Mobilities: Following Indonesian Migrant Workers on Their Way Home (Report)." *Tijdschrift voor Economische en Sociale Geografie* 103 (5): 577–583.

Suryadarma, D., A. Suryahadi, and S. Sumarto. 2012. "Sectoral Growth and Job Creation: Evidence from Indonesia." *Journal of International Development* 25 (4): 549–561.

Suryakusuma, J. I. 1996. "The State and Sexuality in New Order Indonesia." In *Fantasizing the Feminine in Indonesia*, edited by L. J. Sears, 92–119. Durham, NC: Duke University Press.

Tambunan, T., 2007. "Development of SME and Women Entrepreneurs in a Developing Country: The Indonesian Story." *Small Enterprise Research: The Journal of SEAANZ* 15 (2):31–51.

Tickamyer, A. R., and S. Kusujiarti. 2012. *Power, Change, and Gender Relations in Rural Java: A Tale of Two Villages.* Athens: Ohio University Press.

Ukwatta, S. 2010. "Sri Lankan Female Domestic Workers Overseas: Mothering Their Children from a Distance." *Journal of Population Research* 27 (2): 107–131.

Utomo, A. J. 2012. "Women as Secondary Earners: Gendered Preferences on Marriage and Employment of University Students in Modern Indonesia." *Asian Population Studies* 8 (1): 65–85.

Weintraub, A. N., ed. 2011. *Islam and Popular Culture in Indonesia and Malaysia.* London: Routledge.

World Bank. 2011. "Gender Differences in Employment and Why They Matter." In *World Development Report 2012: Gender Equality and Development, ch. 5.* Washington, DC: World Bank. Accessed September 29, 2015. http://siteresources.worldbank.org/INTWDR2012/Resources/7778105-1299699968583/7786210-1315936222006/chapter-5.pdf.

World Bank. 2012. *Picking up the Pace: Reviving Growth in Indonesia's Manufacturing Sector.* Jakarta: World Bank Office. Accessed July 7, 2015. http://www.worldbank.org/content/dam/Worldbank/document/Indonesia-ExecSum-Manufacturing-ENG.pdf.

# Pakistan, Muslim Womanhood and Social Jihad: Narratives of Umm Abd Muneeb

Samina Yasmeen

**ABSTRACT**

Analysts have traditionally ignored women's narratives on jihad and have focused on the views of male jihadists. Research on *Jamat'ud'Dawah* and *Lashker-e-Toiba* fits this pattern, despite the growing involvement of women in the activities of those organizations. This article analyses the narratives and stories, and their implications for the jihadi project with reference to the publications of one female leader in the group, Umm Abd Muneeb. Drawing upon her publications in Urdu, the article explores her discussion of *ḥayā* (modesty), *purdah* (seclusion) and male superiority, and how these ideas are designed to guide women into accepting the need for jihad by male members of their families. The article establishes that ideas of piety are often linked to the political project in narratives of Muslim women affiliated with jihadi groups and that it is necessary to understand the language used by these women in their particular socio-political environment. Such understanding provides a holistic view of how women support and sustain jihad within the family environment.

## Introduction

The post-9/11 era has been marked by a proliferation of literature on jihad and political Islam (see, e.g. Azzam 1993; Burr and Collins 2006; Marranci 2006; Bonner 2006; Neighbour 2009; Springer, Regens, and Edger 2009). The global focus on terrorism and counter-terrorism is reflected in accounts of the origins and ideas promoted by Muslim militant movements around the world (Azzam 1993; Nusse 1999; Robinson 2004; Early 2006; Chehab 2007; Tankel 2011). The discussion invariably remains limited to the ideas and narratives popularized by male members of these movements. Women's agency in jihad (war against unbelievers) and their ideas remain relatively unexplored, with the primary focus being on women's participation in social Islamist groups and circles. Those who do delve into Muslim women's role in jihad often draw upon writings by Muslim men on the issue (Cook 2005), or focus excessively on the phenomenon of female suicide bombers. The trend is slowly changing with literature that draws upon Muslim women's narratives on jihad and its meaning in the contemporary world. The areas span female contestations of their role as combatants in jihad (Lahoud 2014), focus on women's 'jihad of words' with reference to Shi'ite tradition (Hamdar 2009), privileging of organizational rigor and commitment over martyrdom in domestic politics jihad (Haq 2010), and narratives of mothers of *Lashker-e-Toiba* (Army of the Pure) (LeT) martyrs as a means to continued mobilization and recruitment (Haq 2007).

Within the context of the paucity of gender-specific coverage of jihad at a time of heightened sensitivity to jihadi discourses, this article is premised on the understanding that a holistic appreciation of the dynamics of jihad necessitates increased focus on women's agency and their narratives. These narratives, located within the context of the family as the primary unit of human society, provide the norms to engender acceptance of jihad as a *farḍ* (duty) for all members of the family and the community. The process exists parallel to the creation and dissemination of narratives by male jihadi members that provide the parameters within which Muslim women operate to perform their role of connecting 'piety to politics' and creating an 'Islamic habitus' (Mahmood 2004; Deeb 2010). Female leaders affiliated with *Jamat'ud'Dawah* (Organization for Preaching; JuD)[1] in Pakistan reflect this trend and contribution by creating female-oriented literature on jihad. This article provides insight into narratives popularized by one of these women, Umm Abd Muneeb, who focuses on personal piety as part of a social jihad, which contributes to a jihad narrative worth supporting by women, thus rendering it a 'piety to politics' project.

The article's argument is located within the context of narratives, and their possible linkage with promoting certain types of actions. It is developed in four parts: the first discusses the jihadi narratives developed by JuD; the second discusses the typology of female narratives in JuD; the third focuses on the ideas promoted by Umm Abd Muneeb with reference to selected publications within the context of female agency in JuD, and the last discusses the relevance of these narratives for the jihad project being promoted by the organization.

## Jamat'ud'Dawah and the jihad narrative

Narratives as communicators of ideas provide an insight into the perceptions of the narrators as well as into their relationship to the situation under discussion. In the process of the narration, a story is created and communicated that enables the listener or the subject of the narration to gain some understanding of the values and preferences of the narrator. Scholarly literature on how this phenomenon unfolds and could be analyzed has proliferated in the last three decades. No longer limited to literary space, it has been acknowledged as the communicator of perceived and/or portrayed identities. This process, by its very nature, also involves aspects of construction of identity through narration, as well as vision and ideas for the future relationship between the narrator, the situation, and the world as it may evolve. Basil Bernstein (cited in Goodson 2013, 69–70) distinguishes between the codes used for narrative as 'restricted' or 'elaborated'. Linked to a 'hierarchy of competences', the restricted code in his opinion is 'local, de-contextualized and specific'. The elaborated code, on the other hand, is 'more theorized, abstract and contextualized, and [gives] access to wider understanding'. Goodson questions this distinction and argues that 'narrativity needs to be linked to identity, learning and agency if we are to understand its complex social significance'. He argues that:

those following a more descriptive mode can be as agentic and as purposeful in their learning and identity projects as those with a more elaborated style of narrativity. Both modes have action potential, identity potential and learning potential, and it is through the analysis of these potentialities rather than the characterization of narratives as descriptive or elaborative that we come to understand these complex social significances. (69–70)

Striano (2012, 153) further modifies this idea and argues that narratives are intended as 'a form of negotiation and active participation in social discourse and as a way of constructing new social discourses, which develops through a process of on-going and interactive construction (versus fixed and organized narrative formats)'. Hammack (2011, 313) focuses on the political aspects of narratives and argues that the continuous use of narrative by individuals coexists at another level with 'the master narrative … which represents a collective storyline which group members perceive as compulsory – a story which is … central to the group's existence and "essence"'. This suggests, in turn, that, contrary to the views expressed by some analysts, grand narratives have not totally given way to localized narratives and that the grand or master narratives coexist in different spaces with localized narratives, with one feeding into and shaping the other. In other words, as suggested by Halverson, Corman, and Goodall (2011, 23–24), a 'system of stories' emerges that reflects a master narrative.

Jihadi organizations, like all other social movements, tend to develop such master narratives that explain, justify and sustain their respective projects. The studies of ideas of various militants who use Islam as a justification for their actions provide an insight into how these master narratives are constructed and then woven into local narratives (Schaefer 2010; Halverson, Corman, and Goodall 2011; Johnson and Waheed 2011; Sims 2012; Mirbagheri 2012; Long and Wilner 2014). JuD is no exception to this generalized process. Its narrative has been shaped by the dynamics that led to its creation and the support structures that have acted as enablers in its various mutations since the late 1980s. Its origin can be traced to the formal organization of the *Markaz ud-Dawah wal-Irshad* (MDI) in 1986 as the Soviet occupation of Afghanistan was drawing to a close. The Pakistan Army, which has played both a direct and an indirect role in shaping Pakistan's political landscape and determining the parameters of the country's foreign policy, provided the group with initial support and guidance. Building on the experience acquired in the process of pushing the Soviets out of Afghanistan, the Pakistan military had devised a strategy to deal with non-state actors (the jihadi groups) in a bid to wrest control of what Pakistan identifies as 'occupied Kashmir' from India. Chosen as part of the strategy, the MDI established *Lashker-e-Toiba* in February 1990 and initiated a process of mobilization and recruitment of jihadis from within Pakistan (Yasmeen 2005; Tankel 2011). During the 1990s, it engaged in sustained military infiltrations into the Indian part of Kashmir. The LeT also participated in the ill-fated Kargil Crisis (1999) initiated by the then Chief of Army Staff, General Pervez Musharraf, who formally banned the LeT in January 2002 in his capacity as the military ruler of Pakistan. As the beneficiary of the military's sustained support, however, it was able to recreate itself as JuD in December 2001 – weeks before General Musharraf announced the formal ban on LeT. Since then, with the exception of a brief hiatus following the Mumbai bombings of 2008, JuD has operated as a social welfare organization in Pakistan.

Throughout its various mutations, the leadership of JuD has developed a narrative of a symbiotic relationship between *dawah* (preaching) and jihad (holy struggle): while *dawah* draws individuals to jihad, participation in jihad is salvific and promotes 'ethical self-fashioning' (Deeb 2010, 108) and moral reform. Given that the genesis of LeT was linked to a strategy to 'liberate' Kashmir, it is not surprising that the narrative of the group was narrowly focused on the necessity of waging jihad in Kashmir. But the international linkages established during the Afghan war of the 1980s also came to encompass discussion of jihadi activities in regions around the world where Muslims were presented as being oppressed and victimized.

JuD (and LeT in its earlier incarnation) have developed a narrative that explains the support of and participation in Kashmir through the use of scriptures and references to Prophetic tradition. Of these, one of the earliest publications is by Hafiz Abdul Salam bin Mohammad. In a pamphlet entitled *Hum jihad keyon kar rahey hein?* (Why Are We Engaged in Jihad?) (Mohammad 2001), he elaborated on the duty of jihad for all Muslims. He identified jihad as a *fard kifāya* (an obligation for part of the Muslim community) and not *fard 'ayn* (an obligation for the entire community), but emphasized that jihad enabled Muslims to purify themselves and also create conditions for the ultimate victory of Islam over its enemies. This small pamphlet, which was reprinted numerous times by the official publication outlet of the MDI, Dar ul-Andulus, was followed by a number of other publications in the post-9/11 decade. Hafiz Saeed's exegesis of *Sūrat Tawba* (2006), however, remains the most exhaustive and authoritative account of JuD's view of jihad post 9/11. Published while Hafiz Saeed was under house arrest, the exegesis divided human beings into four categories: *munafiqin* (hypocrites), *momineen* (true believers), *ahle kitab* (Christians and Jews) and *kuffar* (unbelievers). The book justified and exhorted people to continue with jihad, despite its identification with terrorism by the West and by enemies of Islam. However, unlike the emerging trend among sections of the Islamist militant movements to target the leadership of Muslim states, the book advised against establishing a conflictual relationship with Muslims. The suggestion was grounded in the Prophetic preference for dealing with *munafiqin* gently to keep the door open for their reform (278–280). These ideas were later repeated in Hafiz Saeed's open letter written to Hamid Mir in 2009 refuting the allegation that he and JuD were behind the Mumbai bombings of 2008. Islam, he argued, forbad people from targeting civilians, and enjoined its followers to abide by strict laws of conflict that did not include unprovoked assault on innocent citizens (Mir 2009).

The jihad narrative presented by male leaders of JuD (and earlier in their capacity as leaders of LeT) primarily targeted male audiences in Pakistan. The securitized religious ideas implied women's agency as supporters of jihad in their roles as mothers, wives, sisters and daughters. These were recurring themes in the obituaries published in *Mujallat ud-dawah*, which narrated the events leading to the martyrdom of members of LeT in the course of jihadi activities, and in the testaments of those martyred, urging their family members and friends to follow the *ahle hadīth* creed and continue on the path of jihad. The reactions of mothers and other female members of the family communicated the persona of women who were prepared to sacrifice their most precious treasures – their sons, brothers and husbands – for jihad. Two factors may explain this gender-privileging narrative of jihad: first, classical Islamic jurisprudence has shied away from identifying and including women as active participants in combat (Cook 2005). Although some radical Islamists have conditionally included women, traditional *'ulamā'* (religious leaders) in Saudi Arabia have been reluctant to condone these re-interpretations of women's role in jihad. The close ideological and political linkages between JuD and Saudi Arabian *'ulamā'*, therefore, could have contributed to excluding women as a direct audience of the jihad narrative. Second, the Pakistan military's role in creating and sustaining LeT as an instrument of its Kashmir policy could also explain why only men were encouraged and mobilized to participate in jihad. As part of the military's strategy of using male fighters in the Indian part of Kashmir, it was essential to develop narratives that mobilized them to engage in jihad but did not necessitate a similar policy vis-à-vis women.

## Emergence of women's narratives

Women emerged as a significant audience for LeT and JuD narratives at the turn of the new millennium. Two sets of events prompted this shift: first, the Kargil Crisis of 1999 resulted in a reassessment of the strategy by members of the group. The involvement of members of LeT in the ill-conceived adventure to wrest control of the Indian part of Kashmir by occupying the mountain ridges above Kargil engaged the international community in May–June 1999, and forced the Nawaz Sharif government to agree to the Washington Accord of July 1999. As part of this arrangement, the Pakistan military and other jihadi groups (particularly LeT) had to withdraw from the occupied Indian areas. The loss of life sustained in the crisis by LeT members prompted the leadership of the MDI to opt for a shift from purely focusing on the Indian threat to creating conditions for changing Pakistan into a truly Islamic society. The metamorphosis from being solely a non-state jihadi group to one that focused on the political project of societal refashioning as a path to jihad necessitated greater focus on women as audience and agents. Second, the shift in the global environment following the terrorist attacks on the USA in September 2001, the attacks on the Indian Parliament in December 2001 that led to the formal banning of LeT in January 2002, and the creation of JuD as a group engaged in *dawah* and social welfare activities within Pakistan necessitated a greater engagement with and focus on women affiliated with JuD.

The increased focus on women's agency has contributed to narratives that target a female audience and mobilize women for both jihad and a political project of societal re-creation – social jihad – with the aim ultimately of guaranteeing Pakistan's success as an Islamic state. The process has occurred in tandem with increased women-specific organizational activities: *Mujallat ud-dawah*, for example, included references to networking among women in its coverage of its annual gatherings (Umm Hammad 2000). The women's wing of LeT became more active than before. *Tayibaat* – a monthly magazine for women – was launched in 1421AH (2000) by MDI; gender-specific literature written by women for women proliferated through the magazine and in the form of books and pamphlets. The narrative included in these publications can be broadly divided into two categories: first, the exaltation of jihad; and second, women's role as agents of social piety in Pakistan. A perusal of the literature published suggests that female leaders affiliated with JuD/LeT have divided the task of popularizing these narratives. Umm Hammad and Professor Umm Abdur Rubb (the editor and assistant editor of *Tayibaat*, respectively) provide an understanding of the global and regional strategic landscape for Pakistan, and the Muslim *umma* (community of Muslims) at large. They focus on the conflict between Islam and its enemies including India, Israel and the West. In October 2003, for example, Umm Hammad, who is married to a senior member of the

MDI, edited obituaries of those who were martyred in Kashmir in three volumes of *Hum maa'ayn Lashker-e-Toiba ki* (We, the Mothers of Lashker-e-Toiba) (Umm Hammad 2003). She has also written poems eulogizing jihad against the enemies of Islam (but not against other Muslims) and reminding readers of the atrocities committed against Muslims around the world. The language used in these accounts of Islam's struggle against the 'other', however, differs slightly from that used for the male audience: there is greater use of stories and anecdotes to draw the reader into the subject matter, rather than high level analysis of developments. An article titled *Yahūd ka mādī, ḥāl wa-mustaq-bil* (The Past, Present and the Future of the Jews), for example, delved into the distortion of historical records and the inaccurate portrayal of prophets such as Dāʾūd (David) and Mūsā (Moses). It claimed that the Jews accuse a descendant of the prophet Dāʾūd of incest, and allege that the prophet Mūsā had intentionally killed a human being (Umm Abdur Rubb 2008). The gender-specific nature of the narrative becomes obvious when compared with the markedly different analyses published in issues of *Mujallat ud-dawah* (2000–2004) that focus on the geo-strategic implications of Jewish conspiracies against Muslims.

The second strand of female narratives are pedagogical in nature: their aim is to rede-fine women's role in a societal sphere as agents that counter the insidious influence of Hindu and Western cultural assault. This is attempted by providing ideas and information that enable the audience (the women) 'to reflect on their environment and social context as well as the … social relationships' (Atkinson 2012, 3) in order 'to engage in a constant process of learning, of "making meaning"' (Santo 2011), of being a good Muslim woman. Umm Abd Muneeb plays a major role in this space. She served as the assistant editor of *Tayibaat* in the past and then occupied the same position in the *Al-Sifat* magazine, which replaced *Tayibaat* after the former was banned in 2008. She has been contributing litera-ture since the turn of the new millennium. The unexplained early death of her daughter, Maryam Khansa, who contributed articles on Islam along with *ahle ḥadīth* creed provided the impetus for her taking on this role. She edited the articles written by Khansa in a book titled *Musalmanon ka fikri aghwa* (The Hijacking of the Muslim Mind) in 2005/2006. Since then she has published a number of small pamphlets targeting the female audience as part of social jihad – reformation of society through female agency. These pamphlets are mostly published by Mushraba Ilm wa Hikmat, not Dar ul-Andulus. They focus on specific social issues, locate them within the context of 'corrupting influences on Pakistani society' and suggest options for dealing with them. Thus, they provide stories that, when read in conjunction with others by Umm Abd Muneeb, create a system of stories that con-tributes to pedagogical narratives. These pamphlets are sold to women through mosques, in *dār*s (study sessions) and also through JuD outlets for men. This article will focus on the stories surrounding concepts of *ḥayā* (reserve and maidenly modesty), *purdah* (female seclusion from men or strangers) and jihad.

## Umm Abd Muneeb and Muslim female piety

Goodson identifies four broad clusters of narrativity and particular types of narrative styles: focused elaborators, scripted describers, armchair elaborators and multiple descri-bers. Of these, 'the major feature of focused elaborators is their concern to break away from inherited scripts or established patterns of socialization' (Goodson 2013, 96).

Though these categories apply to individuals, it could be argued that Umm Abd Muneeb could be identified as a focused elaborator who is writing with a view to encouraging her readers to break away from the inherited scripts of social norms in Pakistan. The idea of inheritance, however, is not located in distant past history but refers to changes that have occurred more recently in Pakistani society and their impact on women's attitudes and behavior vis-à-vis their family members and the wider community (Umm Abd Muneeb 2008b).

Umm Abd Muneeb communicates the need for Muslim women to appreciate the ill effects of societal changes, to protect themselves from these effects in line with early Islamic traditions, and to change themselves in ways that ensure that they become true Muslim women. This is achieved primarily through focusing on three main themes: *ḥayā*, *purdah*, and acceptance of male superiority in private and public spaces alike.

The concept of *ḥayā* in Islam is often translated as modesty, shyness and bashfulness, which may, as reflected in Siraj's discussion of veiling (2011), lead to its erroneous conflation with *purdah* (seclusion). The meaning of *ḥayā* also extends to feelings and emotions linked to modesty. The traditionalists define it as 'a bad and painful feeling accompanied by embarrassment, caused by one's fear of being exposed or censured for some unworthy or indecent conduct' (Haseeb 2010). In the subcontinent, it is also referred to as *sharm* (shame) and *lajja* (Haq 2010). Umm Abd Muneeb discusses the idea of *ḥayā* in a series of pamphlets that refer to Hadiths of the Prophet Muhammad, often narrated by his youngest wife, Aisha, but also by some male narrators. She establishes the authenticity of the idea of *ḥayā* in a pamphlet (2008a, 9–11) from the Hadith narrated by the Prophet Muhammad that urges Muslims 'to control what is between their legs [their private parts] and what is between their jaws [their tongues]'. This is supplemented with evidence provided by the *Ṣaḥāba* (the Companions of the Prophet) that the Prophet Muhammad was as modest as a maiden and would not entertain any immodest idea or discussion (9). These traits, the pamphlets argue, were also adopted by the Rightly Guided Caliphs: Ali, for instance, wanted some advice on a personal matter but modesty prevented him from seeking this advice from the Prophet as Fatima's father. Building on such evidence, Umm Abd Muneeb argues that *ḥayā* is the cornerstone of shaping the character of true Muslim women. They need to observe modesty in how they relate to members of the family, and even those who are close to them. Applying this idea, she further argues that married women need to reflect this modesty in how they relate to their in-laws, and even to their husbands (Umm Abd Muneeb 2008a). These prescriptions are interestingly presented as a continuation of the traditions that existed in the subcontinent prior to the influx of Western ideas and the decay of societal norms.

Umm Abd Muneeb (2009) fully develops the thesis of the need for Muslim married women to observe modesty in their everyday actions in a pamphlet entitled *Ḥifẓ-e-ḥayā aur azdiwaji zindgi* [Protection of Modesty and Married Life]. She argues that Pakistani society has been influenced by Hindu traditions (31–32) and, unlike in the past when girls were trained from their early life to be pious, shy and submissive, contemporary Pakistani women tend to ignore the sanctity of marital relationships. Going to beauty parlors and joking about the impending marriage has become commonplace. Also, the *ḥayā* inherent in a man's relationship with his wife is affected by the tendency to share the most intimate details of their marital lives with friends and family members (14–15).

For Umm Abd Muneeb, the new trend of announcing the impending birth of a child is also against *ḥayā*, and is a deviation from the traditional behavioral norms that prevented women from revealing their pregnancy, even to the *maḥrams* (male relations with whom marriage is prohibited) in their families. Often, the elderly male members did not know until close to the day of the birth that a woman was pregnant, as she would cover herself with a thick chador (2009, 22–23). In contrast, Umm Abd Muneeb points out that, in the contemporary social environment, married women make all members of the family party to the stages of her pregnancy by making early announcements. They start collecting gifts and clothes for the unborn baby instead of following the tradition of handing down clothes from the older babies. These new practices contribute to two evils: they turn pregnancy into a public event and also add to the cost of bearing children. This, in turn, contributes to the discourse of population control:

> In addition to the waste of money, the tendency to buy new and expensive gifts for the expected child also results in popularizing the notion that it is difficult to bear the cost of bringing up children, so that it is sufficient to have only two children. (25; all translations from Umm Abd Muneeb are the author's).

The notion of *ḥayā* also extends to the use of the voice. Drawing upon the Salafi thinking that identifies women as a source of *fitna* (with a capacity to seduce men and cause social instability) and includes the voice as part of the *ʿawra* that must be protected, Umm Abd Muneeb presents a similar argument. In a pamphlet entitled *Awaz ka fitna* (The *fitna* of Voice) published sometime between 2009 and 2011 (Umm Abd Muneeb n.d. a), she claims that the voice has a special link to maintaining and protecting modesty. Referring to the Hadith about keeping control of what is between the jaws, she maintains that people express their emotions and ideas through their voices. The sound of a person's voice, therefore, becomes the expression of that person's nature and personality. But significantly, she argues, the sound also falls under the category of *fitna*: the voice originating from the mouth can lead to sexual relationships prohibited in Islam. The tone of a woman's voice, the inflexion and the softness, therefore, moves women out of the parameters of *ḥayā* and modesty. By implication, modesty requires that women *not* speak softly to others, and should instead maintain an aura so as to avoid the degenerative effects of the '*fitna* of voice'. Women, however, do not shoulder alone the responsibility of ensuring that this *fitna* is contained: Umm Abd Muneeb argues that it is the responsibility of both women and men to control the use of their voices so as to remain within the permissible limits of behavior. With reference to a narration in which the Prophet Muhammad asked a Muslim man to ensure that women in the caravan did not hear his songs, she argues that both genders have a responsibility to carefully maintain the *ḥayā* of voice (67–68).

The *ʿawra* of voice, as suggested earlier, is not a unique concept introduced by Umm Abd Muneeb, as debates have persisted among Islamic scholars as to whether or not 'the female voice is *ʿawra* and should not be heard in public' (Amina n.d.). However, the interesting aspect of her narrative relates to the discussion of how voice travels through sound waves and needs to be contained to remain within the Islamic injunctions of modesty. She argues that songs sung by men or women in public spaces are equally impermissible and must be avoided. Radio and television occupy a special place in this narrative: as communicators of sound, these media provide links with non-*maḥrams* (males with whom marriage is permissible) and must be avoided.[2] However, even more intriguing is her discussion of mobile telephones as agents that impact on the modesty of Muslim women. In an undated pamphlet, *Mobile: Chand khatray ki ghantian* (Mobile: Some Alarm Bells) (Umm Abd Muneeb n.d. b), she argues that voices heard on mobile phones provide a channel of communication with non-*mahrams* and urge them to venture into the arena of prohibited sexual relationships. Using examples from everyday life, she argues that people use mobile phones to connect with other women and chat with them incessantly. This leads them to arrange meetings in person and then engage in un-Islamic practices.

The written word constitutes a further dimension of *haya* in Umm Abd Muneeb's writings. A pamphlet entitled *Hifz-e-haya: Guftagoo aur tehrir* (Protecting *haya*: Conversation and Writing) addresses the nuanced manner in which both speech and writing may affect the morals of Muslim women. She argues that the Qur'an establishes the permissible conventions of communication: the sacred verses clearly indicate the need to discuss human biological needs and realities using implicit and not explicit language. The divine revelation does not use 'even a single word that reflects nudity' (6–7). Marital relationships, she points out, are also discussed in the Qur'an in indirect, modest language, without the use of explicit references to sexual activity. Extending the significance of the written word to those used by human beings, she argues that the Qur'an has emphasized the significance of the written word in the first revelation (Umm Abd Muneeb 2008a). This suggests that human beings have a certain responsibility to use words wisely and modestly. In this context, she places the written word above the spoken word in importance because of the permanence attached to written expressions and their ability to influence people far and wide and across historical periods. She states:

> Spreading the word of Qur'an and Sunnah and promoting piety turns into *ṣadaqa jāriya* [eternal blessing] for a human being. As long as they survive, these writings would guide the human race, and the writer would receive *ajr* (reward) for the words written. In contrast, anyone who popularizes immodesty, deviation from *dīn*, denial of the life after death and vulgar ideas commits a sin (*gunāh*) and would be held accountable for the sin for as long as the writings are read in the world. The writer would also be accountable for anyone who is misguided by reading these writings. (Umm Abd Muneeb 2008a, 36; my translation)

The question as to what constitutes immodesty in writing is further developed when she states that:

> literature, when in the form of poetry and prose, has been used as a weapon by Satan from the start of human existence. Therefore, verses and *ghazals* [love poems], novels and short stories, and now film, drama, (satellite) channels and chatting – all these are the weapons used by the Satan to make us lose our senses. (37; my translation)

Locating this criticism in Prophetic and early Islamic historical tradition, she points out that the Prophet Muhammad strongly condemned the use of vulgar language in literature. The Caliph 'Umar brought in a ban on such language, which was apparent in the prohibition of *tashbīb* – a form of poetry traditionally used by poets to express their love for women by referring to their looks, body shapes and private parts. So strong was his opposition that 'Umar decreed that anyone using *tashbīb* be lashed. Linking *tashbīb* to prevalent literary traditions in Pakistan, Umm Abd Muneeb argues that *ghazal* in Persian and Urdu literature was introduced as a form of *tashbīb*, which essentially condemned it as an impermissible and immodest form of writing. However, instead of singling out *ghazal* as a genre of writing, she claims that:

> in the contemporary era, writers are engaged in using their writings, artistic talents, skills, and the spoken word to spread immodesty and lead people astray. Also those who use their writings, poetry and literature to arouse emotions in the name of depicting reality are following the Satan. (Umm Abd Muneeb 2008a, 40)

*Purdah* as a practice and concept exists for Umm Abd Muneeb in tandem with the idea of modesty. In a pamphlet entitled *Purdah aur khandaan* (Purdah and the Extended Family) published in 2007, she uses the concept of *purdah* interchangeably with hijab and identifies it as an established practice in Islamic societies. The aim of *purdah* for her is to create obstacles on any path that may lead to impermissible relationships between Muslim men and women. Quoting qur'anic verses, she maintains that the divine message has already clearly spelled out the list of male relatives that are *maḥram* and in front of whom Muslim women may display their *zīnat* (beauty). Otherwise, a woman may only show her hands and feet and should conceal the rest of her body and not wear clothes, jewelry, henna, lipstick, kohl, perfume or any other adornments that might make her attractive. Womanly gestures also fall within the purview of *purdah* for Umm Abd Muneeb: she quotes qur'anic verses to support her claim that any *zīnat* that may attract men is not permitted in Islam. The identification of what must be protected from the eyes of non-*maḥram* men leads her to argue that women are required to cover their bodies in a thick chador, and preferably must only talk to men from behind the door. She points out that this would reduce the possibility of any non-*maḥram* males seeing her *zīnat*. *Purdah*, in her opinion, must be observed even among boys as young as 10 years old living within the family home because the information now widely available enables young boys to become aware of women's sexuality earlier than was the case in the past (Umm Abd Muneeb 2007).

These ideas of *purdah* are not unique to the narratives promoted by JuD: Islamist literature abounds in justification for it and an expansive notion of *purdah* with a view to what Deeb (2010, 108) refers to as the 'formation of pious subjectivities and ethical selves through the cultivation of embodied dispositions'. In this connection, Umm Abd Muneeb provides innovative interpretations of the societal changes taking place in Pakistan and their contribution to taking women away from *purdah* – changes that must be resisted for the formation of the ethical self. Telephones, mobile phones and cyberspace are identified as obstacles to women observing *purdah* and maintaining *ḥayā*. The focus reflects the phenomenal appeal of mobile phones and computer technology in Pakistan: according to World Bank Data,[3] the number of mobile users increased from 55% of the population in 2009 to 70% in 2013. The percentage of Internet users also grew from 10% in 2007 to 16% in 2012 (Ameen 2012). Though Pakistan lags behind other countries in Internet usage, the fact remains that mobile phones have become hugely popular, and ownership even extends to poorer sections of society. Despite the changing patterns in the use of technology, Umm Abd Muneeb argues against women having access to mobile phones and for limiting the use of such devices in order to protect the *zīnat* hidden in the sound of their voices. Interestingly, this also extends to ensuring that women do not use ring tones that attract attention, or possess shiny mobile phones that make men look at them.

The concept of *purdah* for Umm Abd Muneeb is closely linked to the notion of men being *qawwām* for women: she consistently reminds women that men are superior to them and so should be respected and submitted to (Umm Abd Muneeb 2009, 19–20). But male superiority also adds to their responsibility of ensuring that women observe *purdah*: male *mahram*s must ensure that women remain indoors, and do not needlessly go out to the market place, where they may speak temptingly with male shopkeepers and be ensnared in sexual relationships. The privileging of the family space for women also has ramifications for the discussion of women's roles in the political, economic and educational spheres. Umm Abd Muneeb questions the right of a Muslim woman to be elected as a member of Parliament, or as the head of a state or even of an organization. Economic rights for women are also questioned with reference to the prevailing unemployment rates in Pakistan: in a society where men have difficulty finding work, she questions the use of women earning their livelihood – especially if it affects the sanctity of family life and impacts on *purdah*. Educational rights for women are also placed at a level below those for men. In a classic statement, she says: 'It is unclear which idiot came up with the idea that girls also need to receive higher education like boys' (Umm Abd Muneeb n.d. a, 61). Her opposition to women operating in the public sphere encompasses their access to health services: she urges women to avoid going to doctors for medical treatment. Instead, as was the case in the past, they should ask male members of the family to communicate their medical problems to practitioners, and be guided by the suggestions for treatment received via the same male relatives.

Effectively, therefore, through a focused narrative, Umm Abd Muneeb is communicating ideas of Muslim womanhood that limit women's agency to the family sphere. Only in limited situations are women permitted to operate in the public sphere, provided they strictly observe *purdah*. Using Goodson's elaboration of focused narrators, one could argue that Umm Abd Muneeb's writings are designed to break away from existing societal practices, and that they promote the idea of reconnecting to the preferred past. Though clearly employing Salafi/*ahle hadīth* codes, the narrative in the publications is not simply linked to the past in the sense of the early Islamic period, but also refers to the norms governing Muslim communities in the subcontinent before the advent of modernization. Her writings do not periodize this past that existed alongside Hindu influence but successfully resisted it and practiced true Islam. Reversion to the past is, therefore, not simply to early Islamic practices but also to early local practices that embodied a restrictive interpretation of women's role in Muslim societies.

The narrative of gender-based role differentiation and the focus on *hayā* and *purdah* could be categorized as part of an agenda for re-selfing and instilling piety among JuD women. As such, it would accord with similar ideas being presented by other Islamist movements in Pakistan such as *Al-Huda*, *Tablīghī Jamaat* and *Jamaat-e-Islami*. Umm Abd Muneeb's narrative, however, links piety to the political project of preparing women as supporters of jihad. Women are encouraged as nurturers to create an environment in which jihad becomes more acceptable in the family and worthy of support. This link becomes apparent in the pamphlets and articles that repeat the information contained in publications for men, but with a female tone. A pamphlet entitled *Tahaffuz-e-nāmūs-e-risālat aur hum* (Guarding Prophetic Sacredness and Us) published in 2011 provides an insight into the link between societal re-selfing and jihad. In tandem with the movement initiated by male members of JuD against blasphemy, this pamphlet urges women to be aware of the need to be vigilant against those determined to blaspheme. Umm Abd Muneeb reminds her readers that demonstrations and condemnations per se do not address the issue. Instead of *ihtijāj* (protest), Muslims need to learn how to focus on *'ilāj* (treatment). Implying that treatment resides in the ability and willingness of Muslims to wage jihad, she argues that Pakistanis have spent eight years celebrating Kashmir Day, and have celebrated Hijab Day and other Days, but have not been able to change the unfavorable situation. The change will come only when societies change, and when the nature of the relationship between Muslims and the non-Muslim world shifts as well. Once Muslim youth cease to be influenced by Western ideas, and are educated in Pakistan instead of overseas, they will be motivated to change society and the international balance. *'Ilāj*, rather than *ihtijāj*, will work. Women have a role to play in this project by helping their children to 'recognize their enemies and the enemies of their nation' (Umm Abd Muneeb 2011).

Women are also reminded of the responsibility to support their men in waging jihad. Even the discussion of the categories of male relatives who are *maḥram* or non-*maḥram* for Muslim women includes the message that the nature of the relationship and affection for their male *maḥram*s must not lead women to stop them from joining jihad.

## Conclusion

The implications of these narratives can be understood with reference to the way we conceive and portray agency in our understandings of the environment we live in and relate to. As stated above, after the Kargil Crisis of 1999, the MDI, and later JuD, shifted away from a one-dimensional focus on jihad against India to one that includes a transformation of both the external and domestic context for Pakistani state and society. This change of focus has resulted in increased emphasis on women's agency in shaping the nature of Pakistani society: Umm Abd Muneeb's narratives form part of a redefined activism for women affiliated with the JuD. In the past they were considered relevant to the overall project for the MDI but were not accorded a significant position in the *jamā'at*'s long-term future. Post-Kargil, however, they have been accorded greater agentic status and have come to be regarded as capable of shifting societal norms directly and the external context indirectly.

It may be argued that Umm Abd Muneeb's focus on *ḥayā'* and *purdah* provides the foundational concepts for the creation of new social structures combined with the uncritical acceptance of men as the *qawwām* of families, and justifies and propagates gender-based role differentiation across society. Women have to be nurturers and submissive to their male counterparts, leaving the public space predominantly under the control of men. This 're-selfing' through the use of narratives is designed to create greater acceptance of unequal roles and rights for women, and different societal norms. The question arises as to how far the narratives have actually achieved this apparent goal.

Haq (2007) is skeptical of the value of the narrative used by LeT to create a particular Islamic female identity and mobilize support for jihad. She considers the pedagogical narratives used in publications, annual gatherings and *dār*s (study circles) insufficient to prompt mothers to sacrifice their sons for the cause of jihad. Combined with her observations of the stern attitudes adopted by female leaders in communicating ideas that may not motivate women sufficiently, she questions the value of written narratives for women in a country with extremely low literacy levels in general and among women in particular. But it could be argued that the knowledge production and communication could result in 're-selfing' among at least some women who are exposed to these ideas. The value of narratives popularized in the form of writings such as those of Umm Abd Muneeb resides in their simplicity and accessibility to women with minimal literacy levels, particularly through the style of writing she adopts: her pamphlets are short, use simple language, refer to ideas and practices that are commonly understood by women, link localized and globalized ideas and norms, and mostly end with a list of 'things to do'. These include how women should observe *purdah*, whom they should talk to, how they should converse with shopkeepers, and how long to spend in the marketplace. The simplicity of these instructions makes them more easily comprehensible, quick to read, and easy to follow. As such, they carry the potential for the audience women to be re-selfed as 'pious Muslims' and become the re-narrators of these ideas. Equally importantly, Umm Abd Muneeb's narratives prepare women to become part of the jihad project carried out by male members of the JuD against India and other enemies of Islam in a manner slightly different from that used by other female narrators of the group.

## Notes

1. Though often identified as Jamaat ud Dawah in literature, this article uses the spelling used by the group's website: http://jamatdawa.com/en/.
2. In this, her views differ markedly from those held in north-western Pakistan, especially in Swat, where radio was used to mobilize both men and women.
3. http://data.worldbank.org/indicator/IT.CEL.SETS.P2 (accessed October 4, 2014).

## Disclosure statement

No potential conflict of interest was reported by the author.

## References

Ameen, Yasir. 2012. "Pakistan Has Highest Growth Rate of Internet Users in Region." *Pulse*, September 28. Accessed October 7, 2014. http://www.aboardthedemocracytrain.com/pakistan-has-highest-growth-rate-of-internet-users-in-region.

Amina, H. n.d. "Is the Female Voice Awrah?" *Muhajabah*. Accessed October 7, 2014. http://www.muhajabah.com/docstorage/voice-amina-h.htm.

Atkinson, Kim. 2012. "Pedagogical Narration: What's It All About? An Introduction to the Process of Using Pedagogical Narration in Practice." *The Early Childhood Educator* 27 (Fall): 3–7.

Azzam, Abdullah. 1993. "What Jihad Taught Me?." In *The Contemporary Arab Reader on Political Islam*, edited by Ibrahim M. Abu-Rabi', 42–47. London: Pluto.

Bonner, Michael David. 2006. *Jihad in Islamic History: Doctrines and Practice*. Princeton, NJ: Princeton University Press.

Burr, J. Millard, and Robert O. Collins. 2006. *Alms for Jihad*. Cambridge: Cambridge University Press.

Chehab, Zaki. 2007. *Inside Hamas: The Untold Story of Militants, Martyrs and Spies*. London: I.B. Tauris.

Cook, David. 2005. "Women Fighting in Jihad?" *Studies in Conflict and Terrorism* 28 (5): 375–384.

Deeb, Lara. 2010. "Piety, Politics and the Role of a Transnational Feminist Analysis." In *Islam, Politics, Anthropology*, edited by Filippo Osella and Benjamin Soares, 107–120. Hoboken: John Wiley & Sons.

Early, Bryan R. 2006. "'Larger than a Party, Yet Smaller than a State': Locating Hezbollah's Place within Lebanon's State and Society." *World Affairs* 168 (3): 115–128.

Goodson, Ivor F. 2013. *Developing Narrative Theory: Life Histories and Personal Representation*. London: Routledge.

Halverson, Jeffry R., Steven R. Corman, and H. L. Goodall, Jr. 2011. *Master Narratives of Islamist Extremism*. Basingstoke: Palgrave Macmillan.

Hamdar, Abir. 2009. "Jihad of Words: Gender and Contemporary Karbala Narratives." *The Yearbook of English Studies* 39 (1/2): 84–100.

Hammack, Philip L. 2011. "Narrative and the Politics of Meaning." *Narrative Inquiry* 21 (2): 311–318.

Haq, Farhat. 2007. "Militarism and Motherhood: The Women of the Lashkar-i-Tayyabia in Pakistan." *Signs* 32 (4): 1023–1046. doi:10.1086/512729.

Haq, Maimuna. 2010. "Talking Jihad and Piety: Reformist Exertions among Islamist Women in Bangladesh." In *Islam, Politics, Anthropology*, edited by Filippo Osella and Benjamin Soares, 156–174. Hoboken, NJ:: John Wiley & Sons.

Haseeb, Zahra Abdul. 2010. "Hayaa' (Shyness)." Accessed October 4, 2014. http://idealmuslimah.com/character/modesty/328-hayaa-shyness.

Johnson, Thomas H., and Ahmad Waheed. 2011. "Analyzing Taliban *taranas* (Chants): An Effective Afghan Propaganda Artifact." *Small Wars and Insurgencies* 22 (1): 3–31. doi:10.1080/09592318.2011.546572.

Lahoud, Nelly. 2014. "The Neglected Sex: The Jihadis' Exclusion of Women from Jihad." *Terrorism and Political Violence* 26 (5): 1–23. doi:10.1080/09546553.2013.772511.

Long, Jerry M., and Alex S. Wilner. 2014. "Delegitimizing al-Qaida: Defeating an 'Army Whose Men Love Death'." *International Security* 39 (1): 126–164.

Mahmood, Saba. 2004. *Politics of Piety: The Islamic Revival and the Feminist Subject*. Princeton, NJ: Princeton University Press.

Marranci, Gabriele. 2006. *Jihad Beyond Islam*. Oxford: Berg.

Mir, Hamid. 2009. "Saeed Slams Suicide Attacks." *The News*, November 27. Accessed October 19, 2015. http://www.pakdef.org/forum/topic/8791-mumbai-attacks/page-52.

Mirbagheri, S. M. Farid. 2012. *War and Peace in Islam A Critique of Islamic/ist Political Discourses*. Basingstoke: Palgrave Macmillan.

Mohammad, Abdul Salam bin. 2001. *Hum jihad keyon kar rahey hein?* [Why Are We Engaged in Jihad?], edited by Markaz ud-Dawah wal-Irshad, 173–273. Lahore: Darul Andulus.

Neighbour, Sally. 2009. *The Mother of Mohammed: An Australian Woman's Extraordinary Journey into Jihad*. Melbourne: Melbourne University Press.

Nusse, Andrea. 1999. *Muslim Palestine: The Ideology of Hamas*. Hoboken, NJ: Taylor & Francis.

Robinson, Glen E. 2004. "Hamas as Social Movement." In *Islamic Activism*, edited by Quintan Wiktorowicz, 112–139. Bloomington: Indiana University Press.

Saeed, Hafiz. 2006. *Tafsīr Sūrat al-Tawba*. Lahore: Darul Andulus.

Santo, Latonya Renee. 2011. "Evaluating Narrative Pedagogy in Nursing Education." DEd. thesis, University of Alabama.

Schaefer, Robert W. 2010. *The Insurgency in Chechnya and the North Caucasus from gazavat to jihad*. Santa Barbara, CA: Praeger Security International.

Sims, Christopher. 2012. "Occidentalism at War: Al-Qaida's Resistance Rhetoric." *Altre Modernità* 8: 206–220.

Siraj, Asifa. 2011. "Meanings of Modesty and the *hijab* amongst Muslim Women in Glasgow, Scotland." *Gender, Place and Culture: A Journal of Feminist Geography* 18 (6): 716–731. doi:10.1080/0966369X.2011.617907.

Springer, Devin R, James L. Regens, and David N. Edger. 2009. *Islamic Radicalism and Global Jihad*. Washington, DC: Georgetown University Press.

Striano, Maura. 2012. "Reconstructing Narrative: A New Paradigm for Narrative Research and Practice." *Narrative Inquiry* 22 (1): 147–154. doi:10.1075/ni.22.1.09str.

Tankel, Stephen. 2011. *Storming the World Stage: The Story of Lashker-e-Taiba.* New York: Columbia University Press.

Umm Abd Muneeb. 2007. *Purdah aur khandaan* [Purdah and the Extended Family]. Lahore: Mushraba Ilm wa Hikmat. Original edition, January/February 2006.

Umm Abd Muneeb. 2008a. *Ḥifz-e-ḥayā: Guftagoo aur tehrīr* [Protecting *ḥayāʾ*: Conversation and Writing]. Lahore: Mushraba ʿIlm wa-Ḥikmat.

Umm Abd Muneeb. 2008b. *Rishtay Keyun nahein miltay?* [Why Are Marriages not Easy to Be Arranged?]. Lahore: Mushraba ʿIlm wa-Ḥikmat. Original edition, 2002.

Umm Abd Muneeb. 2009. *Ḥifz-e-ḥayā aur azdiwaji zindagi* [Protection of Modesty and Married Life]. Lahore: Mushraba Ilm wa Hikmat.

Umm Abd Muneeb. 2011. *Tahaffuzey nāmūs-e-risālat aur hum* [Guarding Prophetic Sacredness and Us]. Lahore: Mushraba ʿIlm wa-Ḥikmat.

Umm Abd Muneeb. n.d. a. *Ta Awaz ka fitna* [The fitna of Voice]. Lahore: Mushraba Ilm wa Hikmat.

Umm Abd Muneeb. n.d. b. *Mobile: chand khatray ki ghantian* [Mobile: Some Alarm Bells]. Lahore: Mushraba ʿIlm wa-Ḥikmat.

Umm Abdur Rubb. 2008. "Yahūd ka māzī, ḥāl wa-mustaqbil" [The Past, Present and Future of the Jews]. *Tayibaat* August: 34–36.

Umm Hammad. 2000. "Khawateen key tarbiyati ijtimāʿat" [Training Sessions for Women]. *Mujallat ud-Dawah* April: 51–52, 54.

Umm Hammad, ed. 2003. *Hum maa'ayn Lashker-e-Toiba ki* [We, the Mothers of Lashker-e-Toiba]. 3 vols. Lahore: Dar ul-Andulus.

Yasmeen, Samina. 2005. "Islamic Groups and Pakistan's Foreign Policy: Lashker-e-Toiba and Jaish Mohammad." In *Islam and the West: Reflections from Australia*, edited by Shahram Akbarzadeh and Samina Yasmeen, 45–62. Sydney: UNSW Press.

# The Malaysian Islamization Phenomenon: The Underlying Dynamics and Their Impact on Muslim Women

Bob Olivier

**ABSTRACT**

Islamization in Malaysia, a Muslim-majority country with a large minority population (approximately 35%) of non-Muslims, has gathered pace over the last 40 years. The process has brought about profound changes in Malaysian society. Drawing upon data gathered through qualitative surveys, the article assesses the views of Malay Muslim women from 'professional classes', or 'elites' on the impact of Islamization on Muslim women in general and those from professional backgrounds in particular. The article also draws upon interviews conducted with Malay men, and non-Malay men and women, to locate the Islamization and Muslim women's narrative in a wider context. It argues that the restrictive effects of Islamization are being felt by Muslim women but are not always articulated in the public space.

This article examines the impact of Islamization in Malaysia on Muslim (largely Malay) women, by exploring narratives of women from the 'professional classes', or 'the elite', in Malaysia. Because this group is highly educated, and because a number of them are actually engaged in activities that involve monitoring and commenting on Malaysian politics and society, their collective views provide some insights as to how the phenomenon is affecting women generally, not only the elite. The article also draws upon interviews conducted with Malay men, and non-Malay men and women, to locate the Islamization and Muslim women's narrative in a wider context. It begins by presenting the conditions that have given rise to the Islamization phenomenon and then provides an indication of how Islamization is affecting day-to-day life in Malaysia. The main body of the article then focuses on how the phenomenon is affecting Muslim women, first in general, and then specifically the elite.

## Background

Malaysia has a population of nearly 30 million, which, according to the most recent national census, is divided roughly into 63% Malay, 25% Chinese, and 7% Indian, with

46

the remainder made up of a variety of indigenous ethnic groups, plus a quite sizeable population of expatriates of all nationalities (Malaysian Department of Statistics 2010). All Malays are Muslims, so with the inclusion of Muslims of other ethnic groups, Malaysia is a Muslim-majority country (more than 65%). Since Independence from Britain in 1957, it has modernized at a very rapid rate, transforming itself from a predominantly planta-tion/mining economy to one that is diversified, but which particularly relies on manufac-turing, and oil and gas. More than half the population live in the large urban centres, and these centres, reflecting the economy, have modernized dramatically, particularly over the last 25 years. With their commercial and residential skyscrapers, international hotels, Western-style restaurants, nightclubs, pubs, and women of all ethnic groups making up about half of the workforce, including many in very senior positions in both government and the private sector, the urban centres, particularly Kuala Lumpur, appear not so differ-ent from typical Western cities. However, outside the urban centres, in the rural areas, which are dominated by Malays, life is far more traditional, and the influence of Islam is far more apparent.

Islam came to what is now termed Peninsula Malaysia in about the thirteenth century, and spread throughout the peninsula by the fifteenth century, so it has had more than 500 years to become fully embedded in Malay society. However, with the strong influence of ancient Malay culture, plus Hindu culture from exposure to the Srivijaya Empire for a few hundred years prior to the rise of the Malacca Sultanate, the Islam practised in Malaysia was quite moderate in comparison with that of the Middle East, notably for the relative equality accorded to women. The Malacca Sultanate, which was set up in the early four-teenth century, and centred on the port of Malacca, became a great commercial success, so much so that it attracted the attention of the emerging European powers, first the Portu-guese, then the Dutch. Between them, these two controlled what is now Indonesia and Malaysia, until the arrival of the British, who took over control of all Peninsula Malaysia in 1824 (Andaya and Andaya 1982).

The effects of colonization by the British, which ended with Independence in 1957, were profound, and reverberate to this day. In the relentless pursuit of their commercial objectives, the British transformed the demography of the country by importing huge numbers of Chinese and Indians to work in their plantations and mines, and relegated the Malays to largely rural activities, thus cutting them out of commercial activities and consequently making them bystanders to the significant economic development that occurred over the next 130 years (Alatas 1977; Kessler 1992). However, the British chose to cultivate the Malay elite, particularly the aristocracy, enrolling them in the civil service, and ensuring that they benefited from the changes that were occurring. They also cultivated the most able and enterprising of the Chinese and Indians, collaborating with them to drive their various commercial ventures. The consequences of these actions were that, by 1957, the Malay proportion of the population had dropped from an overwhelming majority before the British arrived to about 50%, and their share of the economy was less than 2% (Jomo 2004, 9). These two facts are key to what unfolded in Malaysia over the decades that followed, including the Islamization phenomenon.

As with any dramatic social change, it is probably impossible to definitively identify all the factors that were/are involved in the rise and continued momentum of Malaysia's Isla-mization phenomenon, let alone how they interacted and continue to interact. However, a few stand out. First, the race riots of 1969 gave rise to the implementation of the New

Economic Policy (NEP), an affirmative action programme aimed at raising the Malay share of the economy and of professional positions, while also eradicating (or at least reducing) poverty, across all ethnic groups. While sound in principle, and receiving general support, the NEP was poorly implemented, with too many benefits going to too few well-connected Malays. This caused tension between the ethnic groups, as well as between the 'haves' and 'have-nots' within the Malay community, the latter group becoming vulnerable to approaches from Islamists offering solace in religion (Noor 2000). Meanwhile, the modernization that the British had set in motion, and which the government now accelerated with its industrialization programme (and which was later accelerated even further under the premiership of Dr Mahathir Mohamad), together with the urbanization that accompanied it, was having an unsettling effect on the Malays, particularly the males (discussed further below), which was a further reason for looking to religion as a means of 'retraditionalizing' (Othman 2004, 151). Meanwhile, other factors were creating an environment that was becoming increasingly conducive to greater religiosity.

At around the time the NEP was being introduced, a missionary movement known as *dakwah* (from Arabic: *da'wa*) was developing, primarily out of the universities (University of Malaya in particular), in protest against what was perceived as corruption in government, and calling for a return to the basics of Islam, especially with regard to justice and morality (Anwar 1987; Nair 1997). This coincided with a worldwide revival in Islam, which undoubtedly provided some inspiration for the *dakwah* movement, and which was certainly a major contributor to an unintended consequence of the NEP. A key objective of the NEP was to increase the number of Malays in professional jobs, and to this end thousands of young Malays were sent to overseas universities, in a wide variety of countries, both in the West, and in the Middle East and South Asia. The majority of these students were from rural areas and they suddenly found themselves far from home, in many cases unable to speak the language of the host country. They were thus vulnerable to being inducted into strongly religious groups, and becoming far more religious than they had been when they left Malaysia. These students returned to Malaysia and, like the *dakwah* group, became advocates in their home communities and workplaces for an increase in religiosity (Ong 1990, 267).

Giving further impetus to an increase in Islamic religiosity was the rise of the *Ketuanan Melayu* concept, which is about clearly establishing the Malay identity, delineating Malays from the rest of the Malaysian population, and asserting their claim to be the original inhabitants of the country, and consequently their rights to special privileges (Shamsul 2001; Kessler 2014). The Constitution, and later the NEP, had defined 'Malayness' as possessing a number of features, but over time it appeared that the definition was becoming a little blurred. As Judith Nagata (1980, 409) explains: 'Malay[ness] no longer provides a sufficient distinction between Malays and non-Malays as a basis for ethnic identity. The erosion of the first two elements of "Malayness" – language and *adat* (Malay custom) – has left only one effective distinguishing feature – Islam.' Not only has this served as a motivation for individual Malays to become more overtly Islamic, but it has also, as Nair (1997, 22) argues, been co-opted by politicians to equate 'protection of Islam' with 'protection of the Malays'.

The 22 years of the premiership of Dr Mahathir Mohamad (1981–2003) gave the Islamization phenomenon a massive boost in a number of ways. He oversaw the development of a version of Islam that emphasized particular behaviours to suit his objectives (for example, ethical conduct in the service of government, and seeing economic success as compatible with Islam), the setting up of religious institutions within government to administer the practice of Islam on a national basis, and the recruitment of large numbers of clerics (*ulama*) into those institutions, many of whom were the returning students mentioned earlier (Wain 2009). These *ulama*, many of whom had studied in Egypt, Saudi Arabia, Iran and Pakistan, were schooled in a version of Islam that was more 'traditional' even than that which had previously been the norm in Malaysia (which was already quite a traditional version), and they reflected this schooling in their administration (Mohamad 2009). Mahathir essentially set up the infrastructure via which the government's version of Islam could be systematically disseminated to the Malay population, and adherence to it enforced, with all the power of the State behind it (Nair 1997).

Joseph Liow (2003) establishes that, having created this powerful infrastructure, Mahathir then fell victim to the accusations of his main political foe, the Pan-Malaysian Islamic Party (PAS) (an Islamic party that has consistently, to the present day, advocated the setting up of an Islamic state in Malaysia), that the government was not doing enough to promote Islam, setting off a 'race' between the two parties (Mahathir's United Malays National Organization [UMNO] and PAS) as to which was the most Islamic. Given the infrastructure described above, and given that the government has up to now been in an almost unassailable position, this race has seen the Islamization stakes raised higher and higher, probably far beyond what the UMNO politicians themselves ever intended, but still not as far as PAS would like to see.

The factors described above are the dominant determinants of Islamization, which is inherently a very complex phenomenon. There are undoubtedly many others, including international events that have the effect of Malays identifying with Muslims elsewhere who are undergoing hardships. These include the invasions of Afghanistan (2001) and Iraq (2003), the Israel/Palestine situation, and the repression of the Muslim Brotherhood in Egypt. Other international events have had an inspirational effect on Muslim populations around the world, including Malaysia, in particular the Iranian Revolution in 1979, and the Islamic revival that is occurring in Turkey. There are also other factors in Malaysia, such as the infiltration of more traditional Islamic thinking via the funding by Saudi Arabia of mosques and religious schools, and the rise of NGOs that aggressively promote Malay rights, often using Islam as the vehicle. Finally, and significantly, there is the fact that there is very little opposition to what is happening, for reasons I shall touch on shortly.

## Manifestations of Islamization in Malaysia

The changes that are associated with the rise of the Islamization phenomenon are most apparent in the urban centres, particularly Kuala Lumpur. Anyone who was familiar with the city over 25 years ago would immediately notice a number of superficial differences: most of the Malay women are wearing *tudungs*, which was not the case previously; on Fridays the mosques are so full that the roads surrounding them are almost impassable; the call to prayer announced through loudspeakers has significantly increased in volume; and almost all the traffic policemen are Malays. A visit to a government department would reveal that virtually all the staff are Malays. At government evening functions attended by many foreigners, where previously alcohol was served, today it has been replaced by a non-alcoholic syrup drink. Even in Western-style restaurants, the number of Malays drinking wine would be minimal. Other changes are more profound.

For a country that has promoted itself as a paragon of multiracial harmony (epitomized by the highly successful 'Malaysia Truly Asia' tourist advertisements), there has been a gradual but significant separation of the ethnic groups. This has been brought about by two major factors, one direct, and the other indirect. The first is that Islamization has brought about an obsession on the part of Malays with ensuring that there is not even the slightest chance that they come into contact, in even the most indirect way, with pork (Frith 2001). They will generally not go to any restaurant that serves pork, on the basis that the dishes and utensils may have been contaminated. Increasingly, they will not go to dinner at a Chinese family's home, for the same reason. Given that a great deal of interaction between people occurs while dining, and the fact that non-Malays often like to frequent places that provide pork, and like to drink alcohol, a major opportunity for interaction is disappearing. A number of my Chinese research participants recounted stories of Malay friends with whom they went to university in the UK slowly drifting away from them, to the point that they now virtually never see each other.

The second factor is an indirect result of the politicization of Islam, in the context of promoting *ketuanan Melayu*. For example, the education system has strongly favoured Malays, to the extent that they represent the vast majority of attendees at government-provided schools and universities. At government schools, the curriculum is largely conducted in Malay, and is increasingly influenced by Islam (Barr 2010). Those non-Malays who can afford it attend private schools, and at university level many either go overseas or attend private universities. The result is that the ethnic groups begin to be separated from early school age, again in great contrast to the situation 30 or 40 years ago, when all ethnic groups were generally educated together in government schools, where, according to most of my research participants, there was little consciousness of one's ethnic group or religion. In addition, the more strident of the *ketuanan Melayu* advocates, generally found in NGO's such as Perkasa and Isma, react harshly and provocatively to the slightest perception of a threat to Islam by non-Muslims. The most recent example (a current issue) concerns the use of the word 'Allah' in Christian Bibles in places such as East Malaysia, which has resulted in accusations of threatening Islam and confusing the Malays, and consequent court cases. Periodically (in recent years) there have been accusations, always shown subsequently to be unfounded, that Malays are being converted to Christianity in large numbers. Such situations sour relations between the ethnic groups, resulting in further separation.

Religion is now impacting on the private lives of Malays, with religious police at federal, state and local council level ensuring adherence to various regulations, such as attendance at Friday prayers; fasting during Ramadan; not drinking alcohol; and single people not being allowed to be alone with a member of the opposite sex. In Malay society generally, there is less tolerance than there was formerly for any behaviour deemed 'un-Islamic'. For example, one of the Malay males interviewed for the project commented that one could not even be safe drinking alcohol at a private party, as someone might innocently post a photo on Facebook, resulting in widespread disapproval. Increasingly, one sees in the press strident calls for strict adherence to Islamic norms from youth groups and Islamist NGOs. Such calls are clearly reinforced by the religious authorities, as evidenced by an article published in *Malay Mail Online* – a well-known online website – on 31 July

2014. Under the heading 'Malaysian Muslims facing fascist indoctrination, former minister says,' it reported: 'The former de facto law minister cited as example the Hari Raya sermon by the Malaysian Islamic Development Department (Jakim), where Muslims were told to reject liberalism, capitalism, pluralism, secularism, materialism and modernity.' The Editor of *The Star* on 3 August 2014 addressed the same issue, under the heading: 'Some right-wingers have gone to ridiculous lengths to promote their narrow-minded views.' Interestingly, around the same time, *The Star* launched a campaign that promoted a number of key values, including democracy, moderation, and tolerance. Given that *The Star* is closely aligned with one of the government coalition parties, it is possible that this was an attempt to dampen down what was becoming an increasingly intolerant and confrontational public conversation.

## Impact on Muslim women in general

### Women and Islamic revivals

Women being placed at the forefront of efforts to re-establish cultural identity in post-colonial and Islamizing societies is a recurring theme. Leila Ahmed (1992, 164) has asserted that:

> The veil came to symbolize in the resistance narrative, not the inferiority of the culture and the need to cast aside its customs in favour of those of the West, but, on the contrary, the dignity and validity of all native customs, and in particular those customs coming under fiercest colonial attack – the customs relating to women – and the need to tenaciously affirm them as a means of resistance to Western domination.

Farish Noor (2000, 11), writing about post-colonial societies, has drawn attention to a return to familiar tropes and markers of communitarian identity such as the veil, and that it is often the case that the weakest sections of such societies (women, children, the peasantry and labourers) are the ones who are forced to carry the burden of maintaining a sense of particular, authentic cultural identity for the sake of the nation as a whole.

Sisters in Islam (SIS), an NGO whose objective is to stand up for the rights of Muslim women in the face of the Islamization phenomenon, in their publication *Muslim Women and the Challenge of Islamic Extremism*, made the same point (Othman 2005). It would also appear that, in the process of reclaiming cultural identity, the implementers (invariably men), generally choose a path that sees the rights of women reduced. Farida Shaheed (2004, 13), who in this same context refers to women as being 'frequently made the repositories of culture', points out that

> whenever an option is provided by a conflict between religious doctrine, customary practices, or state law, the one least favourable to women, the one offering them the least rights, is the one that will most likely be implemented. This tendency signals that the desire to control women is the primary motivation that informs patriarchal authority in these decisions, not religious or other considerations.

### Historical treatment of Malay women

Aihwa Ong (1990) carried out significant research into the role of women in traditional Malay society prior to colonization, and found that it contrasted significantly with the situation that she encountered in the 1980s. She found that in those days, while the largely rural Malays were very religious, they followed a version of Islam that was quite influenced by traditional Malay culture. Women worked alongside their men in the fields, and generally women had a certain degree of economic independence. Females generally inherited an equal share of land with their male siblings, and not the lesser share that was generally the case in Islamic societies. Lily Rahim (2006, 3) shares this view and argues that:

> In contrast to the generally subordinate status of Arab women particularly in pre-Islamic times, Southeast Asian women have traditionally enjoyed relatively high social status and access to public space. *Adat* (traditional and customary) laws bestowed both sons and daughters equal rights to the family property. Such laws also provided that all property acquired during marriage was divided equally in the event of a divorce.

Ong (1990, 260) concludes:

> Malay society is often cited as an example of a Muslim society that permitted relatively egalitarian relations between the sexes (Djamour 1959; Firth 1966; Swift 1963; Wazir-Jahan 1988 [a text apparently held by Ong]; Kabeer 1988), compared, say, with the rigid gender segregation found in Bangladesh (Kabeer 1988). However, in the post-independence period, forces linked to economic development and Islamic revivalism have undermined the *adat* emphasis on bilaterality while strengthening Islamic tenets that increase male control over domestic resources.

Notwithstanding the above observations, in traditional Malay societies men were the undisputed masters of their households, and were not at all threatened by their womenfolk having a fair degree of freedom. Ong presents in detail how the Malay family and surrounding *kampung* society operated, in particular the role played by both Islam and traditional Malay culture (*adat*), and then, after describing the destabilizing effect of colonization with its accompanying immigration and modernization, makes a critically important observation:

> In *kampung* society then, Islamic law defined a man's identity in terms of his ability to prepare his sons for independent house-holding, to control the sexuality of his wife and daughters, and to provide all economic support for his household. However, *adat* practices and kindred relations provided women a measure of autonomy and influence in everyday life that prevented a rigid observation of male authority. In recent years, state policies and capitalist relations have created conditions that make the regulation of female sexuality a major issue. The possibilities for interracial liaisons created by the interweaving of Malay and non-Malay worlds have been perceived as a threat to Malay male rights and as a dangerous blurring of boundaries between Muslim and non-Muslim groups. … control over female sexuality has been made a focus of the resulting efforts to strengthen male authority, reinforce group boundaries, and ensure the cultural survival of the Malay community undergoing 'modernisation'. (Ong 1990, 262)

## The impact of the evolution of Sharia family law

Since Independence in 1957, there has been an increase in the extent of codification and standardization of Sharia law, particularly regarding family law, which has included an increasing trend towards lowering the status of women, and reducing the protections afforded them. Maznah Mohamad (2014), citing numerous academic studies including Hooker (1976), Oba (2002), Yeger (1979), Anwar (2001, 2008), Horowitz (1994),

Peletz (2002) and Noriani Nik Badli Shah (2008), describes how the process has evolved through stages that, in her view, have successively enhanced a 'masculine bias'. 'It has moved from being "women-friendly" in the 1970's to more ambivalent and questioning of women's legal gains in the 1980's and eventually an exclusive "male-domain-of-privilege" in the 2000's' (Mohamad 2014, 177).

Family law within Sharia was initially codified, to some degree, during the British colonial era, and reflected, as well as the Qur'an, both Malay custom and Western law. Thus, it essentially retained the relative freedoms for Malay women described earlier. Notwithstanding further codification and consolidation both before and after Independence, this situation remained much the same until the 1980s. In 1984, the Federal Government oversaw a major revision, which included a significant expansion in the scope of family law (the number of provisions increased from 25 sections to 135), but which was still quite generous in its attitude to women. Then, during the 2000s, a further major revision took place, which essentially replaced the 1984 statutes with others that Mohamad (2014, 183) says 'enhanced men's entitlements and curtailed women's rights.' To give just one example: in the earlier statutes, while polygamy was legally permitted, the conditions imposed for it were very difficult to meet – the living standard of a man's first wife and children could not be lowered, and he had to prove that the new marriage was both necessary and just. In the revision, these requirements were watered down considerably, and in addition, the punishment for an illegal polygamous marriage was quite light. It is now relatively easy for a man to get permission to take an extra wife (or wives), even if he has limited financial means to maintain them.

It would seem that Ong (1990) was quite prescient. The changes that have been made to Sharia family law in recent times do indeed appear to have had the effect of enhancing male authority. Not only do they ensure that male rights are conferred, but they also demand that women's rights 'are constructed around conditional clauses of loyalty, obedience, purity and subservience' (Mohamad 2014, 185). Ong also goes on to contend that Islamic judges tend to favour men in their court rulings, an observation corroborated by many of my research participants. For example, a Malay woman related to me a case in the 1990s in which a friend of hers, a female lawyer, appearing in court with severe bruising on her face and seeking a divorce, was told by the judge that she must have provoked her husband. The strong impression I have gained from many conversations with both male and female Malays is that a woman who is not financially independent is very vulnerable if there is a breakdown in her marriage.

## Day-to-day impact of Islamization

The changes to family law described above are probably the most significant in terms of their potential to have a very major impact on Muslim women, but of course this only occurs in the event of an actual breakdown in their marriage. However, Mohamad (2014) also makes the point that the relative ease with which men can divorce their wives, and perhaps avoid the financial consequences, constitutes a continuing threat hanging over the heads of more vulnerable women, even if it never actually takes place. These observations were borne out in the response by a female respondent (a Malay academic) I interviewed, who said that a lot of middle-class Malay women were unconcerned about increasing Islamization until they actually had to contend with the Sharia courts, and then they rapidly changed their minds. But there are also other ways in which the Islamic revival has affected women in their day-to-day life.

First, religiously inspired intrusion into private life as described above has affected both sexes (with regard, for example, to drinking alcohol, breaking fasting rules, being caught with a member of the opposite sex who is not a spouse or relation). However, a number of respondents (both males and females) suggested that the enforcement of these restrictions seems to be more rigorous in the case of women. When asked why, the males said that the religious police were reluctant to tackle men, but did not offer a reason. Then, there is the fact that most Malay women now wear a head-covering. This is a relatively recent phenomenon, which is driven by a variety of factors, including very significant peer pressure, encouragement from spouses and other family members, and reinforcement by the religious authorities (Nagata 1984; Anwar 1987; Martinez 2000). However, it would appear that personal conviction is also a major factor: according to a large survey conducted in the mid-2000s, 99% of Malaysian women believe veiling is an Islamic duty (Hassan 2008).

The changes to family law described above created conditions that made it easier for men to have more than one wife, and predictably, polygamy is on the rise, at all levels in the community. Miriam Zeitzen (2001), in a research project into polygamy among the Malaysian elite, confirmed that it is indeed increasing, for a variety of reasons, including: the fact that, with the rapid growth in the economy, combined with the effect of the NEP, many Malays have accumulated considerable wealth, and for some, taking additional wives is a sign of success ('trophy wives'); the increase in religiosity makes it more acceptable than in the previously more secular and more Western-influenced environment. SIS has recently conducted a major survey (soon to be published) into the situation regarding polygamy in Malaysia. They have expressed great concern about the fact that polygamy has indeed risen significantly, and that this is having a harmful effect on many of the women involved, including financial hardship and the emotional stress and hurt that invariably accompanies polygamy.

One respondent pointed out that the focus on personal piety was also present among middle-class female professionals. She likened this phenomenon to 'an obsession with sin' and maintained that this 'obsession' could even extend to issues of personal grooming, giving rise to questions such as whether plucking eyebrows, or wearing lipstick, is a sin. The interviews suggested the focus on female piety emerging as a concern among some men as well. The husband of a very senior professional Malay woman, who refused to wear a head-covering, was concerned about her not subscribing to 'Islamic dress code'. She allayed his concerns by, in her words, telling him that she had 'taken the sin from his shoulders and taken it upon herself'.

Notwithstanding all the above, Malay women appear to enjoy relatively equal status with men in the public sphere. The Constitution grants women (irrespective of their ethnicity) the right to vote. Moreover, women have full access to education, more women attend university than males, and Malay women have similar representation at university to that of women of other ethnicities (Rajaendram 2014). While the representation of women in the workforce is relatively low, at about 48%, Malay women are as well represented as the other ethnic groups (Ministry of Women 2014). They are well represented in the professions and the upper levels of business, both private and public. For example, the head of the Central Bank is a Malay woman, as was the previous head of the Securities

Commission. Recently, there has been a major push for at least 30% of all board members to be women. This all looks very positive and encouraging for women. But it would appear that two opposing forces are at work, because at the same time much of the rhetoric associated with the Islamization phenomenon has patriarchal overtones, with the associated connotations of reducing the status of women.

## Narratives of the urban professional class/elite Muslim women

The sample collected for this research includes a subset of Malaysians (all races, and both genders) who are well educated and well-travelled, have extensive exposure to Westerners, and are generally occupying the more senior roles in the community (business, academia, journalism, politics, etc.) – one might term them the elite or the professional classes. The aim of the research was to probe this group's response to the Islamization phenomenon, via face-to-face interviews with approximately 100 people. To date over 90 have been interviewed, and 20 of these are Malay (Muslim) women. All of the latter are professionals: 18 of them are still employed, one is retired but serving on a number of listed company boards, and one is retired but still active in academic pursuits. All 20 take their religion seriously, and generally adhere to the basic rituals of Islam. Feeling that the quality of religious instruction available is generally poor, most of them have undertaken their own study of Islam, to determine for themselves what the Qur'an did and did not say, rather than blindly accepting what supposed experts told them.

My first priority was to establish this group's broad response to the Islamization phenomenon; whether they approved or disapproved, and why. In summary, while over half of the Malay women interviewed felt that a greater awareness of religion in their society was a positive thing, all 20 were unanimous in their disapproval of the more extreme manifestations that are accompanying increased Islamization in Malaysia. They were generally quite scathing about many of the manifestations described above, and most are at the very least apprehensive about how much further Islamization will proceed, and how much more extreme it may become. Overall, 11 disapproved unreservedly, 3 disapproved but with qualifications, 4 approved, but again with qualifications, and 2 approved unreservedly. These two felt that the more extreme manifestations, while they personally felt they were unpalatable, were a small price to pay for the general benefits to Malay society that Islamization would bring. In fact, one said she would welcome Malaysia becoming an Islamic state, including the implementation of ḥudūd punishments, and the other said she would not be concerned at that prospect. An interesting revelation from the first of these was her relating the setting up of an Islamic state to the political unification of all the Malays, and her conviction that this was desirable and necessary.

Some brief quotes from a number of these women on this specific question give an indication of their thinking (all names are pseudonyms):

> Noraini: Actually, I'm not comfortable. … Religion should sit closely with values. What I'm seeing is religious practices, (rather than values). Maybe our values are not aligned, I'm not really too sure. The values seem to be deteriorating rather than improving, over the years, a common observation. It's even worse when religion is politicized, and I'm not comfortable with it.

> Hamidah: It makes me very wary.

Saleha: I'm strongly against it. It's invasive, and it's putting pressure on me that I don't want.

Jamilah: In some ways it's good, in some ways it's a bit odd. Greater consciousness about religion is good, but the way some things are imposed is not so good. It should be between you and God.

Azizah: It's the mindset that's changed, the attitude to religion. People have become much more insular in their views. There's a lot of peer pressure, people affected by what other people think. A cultural change (way of life – what you wear, what you do, drink, go out, … ), then the whole political change. Islam is so much more prevalent in politics. The political game has mobilized people, the whole movement has become bigger, and transformed into a social movement.

Zubaidah: It's gone political, and once you get politics in it, it gets messed up. So if you're a Muslim you think you have to cover up, and they have all these silly laws, like not being allowed to drink in public, and religious police breaking into hotel rooms.

Jamilah: I think Islamization is something that was bound to happen – it's what kind is the issue. It was inevitable because of post-colonization, to attach to the bigger Muslim community. It has a lot to do with self-esteem. … One of the bad things is that Islamization was not organic – too government driven, and too Arabized.

Anis: Not sure whether I approve or disapprove. It's real, for sure. … But the phenomenon is worrying.

Fauziah: At the end of the day, I don't really care. … If the country really goes down that path, I can walk.

While most of these women have, at the least, reservations about the Islamization phenomenon, it does not appear to have directly impacted on them much more than it has on their male counterparts. However, the issue of veiling surfaced in the interviews as one area of piety that impacted on the respondents' participation in the public space. Though veiling was not the criterion used for selecting the respondents, as it happens only one of them wore the Islamic head-covering, and identified it as reflecting her personal conviction rather than the result of any form of coercion. Other respondents shared the view that wearing the veil is obligatory in Islam but they had chosen not to do so. Some of them reported coming under some pressure to alter their dress code to coincide with public perceptions of piety. A number of them reported that their children, if they went to a government school, came under great pressure to cover, at a quite young age, and this concerned them.

Saleha: My two daughters were questioned at school about their mother not wearing a *tudung*. The teacher said not to take any notice of what I said because I was not a good Muslim. So, I removed them from the school.

Of course, this group has the financial ability to do this – not all Malay women would have that choice. Some other comments concerning veiling:

Noraini: A simple one: Why are the women covered? It's really the men's problem – they can't control themselves.

Anis: I want to see more substance than form in religion. If someone looks at me then they wouldn't think that I'm religious, but I am. I don't wear a *tudung*, and I'm sleeveless, so they just dismiss me. So, the bad thing is the judgement.

In fact, it appears that their position in society, which is generally accompanied by at least financial 'comfort', has shielded this group from the more extreme manifestations of the Islamization phenomenon. A number of them actually said that they were not at all concerned about it, as it just did not affect them. For example, they are better able to deal with the difficulties often presented by the Sharia courts than less well-off women, who are often completely financially dependent on their husbands. (This group was not even aware of the changes to family law described above.) One of them commented: 'What's the problem? When I got divorced I just paid him off and got rid of him – it was easy!' The enforcement of adherence to religious norms seems to pass them by – it was explained to me by a number of my male Malay participants that the religious police, while they do target working-class Malays, particularly the women, avoid the elite group.

Nevertheless, some of the participants objected in principle to the concept of religious police enforcing Islamic norms, and societal pressure to conform:

Azizah: What upsets me is that people's mindset is so religious – most of them. I bet it's very rare to find any senior person who would openly do what they often do privately. Fasting is a very good example. No one dares to not adhere to this.

Zubaidah: I think that it violates privacy. What you do between you and your God is your business. To be picked up by the police for having a glass of wine is not what I think Islam is about.

Zaleha: It's so religiously suffocating here that I'm going back to the UK, for good.

One issue that apparently does affect this group of women, although not the specific women I interviewed, is polygamy. A number of my participants, both male and female, said that they believed polygamy had increased, and this is corroborated by Miriam Zeitzen's research. She estimates that only 2–3% of marriages in Malaysia are polygamous, but that the incidence among the elites is much higher (Zeitzen 2008, 71). At an SIS symposium in Kuala Lumpur on 8 January 2013, when speaking on the topic 'Polygamy among urban elites in Malaysia', she stated that the incidence of polygamy among the elites was increasing. One of my male participants, who has more than one wife, was honest enough to confirm that one of Zeitzen's conclusions, that the accumulation of wives was a sign of having 'made it', was indeed true. SIS, an NGO composed of a small group of well educated women who are activists for women's rights, are currently working on a report on polygamy, motivated by their concern about its rise in the general Malay community. One of my participants had this to say on the subject:

Zubaidah (during a discussion as to whether men were taking advantage of the increased Islamization): Yes, some that I know have. Because it suits them, and I see it happening more and more, because it's allowed, it's more acceptable. It's embarrassing for Islam, the non-Muslims laugh at us.

While some of my female Malay participants may be rather sanguine about the Islamization phenomenon, believing that they are not personally affected because they are above it all, others are apprehensive about what may happen in the future. A number of my participants, both male and female, commented on how 'Arabized' Malaysia was becoming (one of them actually said: 'What's happening in Malaysia is not so much Islamization, as Arabization.'), a trend that is understandably disturbing to women who are used to a moderate environment. While only one of the participants is convinced that Malaysia is heading towards becoming an Islamic state, 8 of them believe it is a definite possibility. Fifteen of them believe that the Islamization trend is definitely going to continue, and two more believe it may well continue. Some of their thoughts on this follow:

Azizah: The Founding Fathers' vision is dying. And when that dies, what happens? The fundamental Malays are dominating. I'm not sure we'll end up as an Islamic state, but it's very worrying nevertheless.

Anis: Because women's rights are being suppressed more now than before. There are more divorces, and women are being treated badly. The family unit was more cohesive, and there was more family protection for women.

Zaitun: Where is Islamization going to end up? I don't think it will go to extremes, like Saudi, or Iran. There's enough of a multicultural society to arrest it. Chinese and Indians are a big part of the economy – the country couldn't survive without them. If they suddenly weren't there we'd die. They were the catalyst for our economy. My hope is that my generation and the next generation, there will be enough educated Malays to be sensible about religion, and not allow it to go to extremes.

Noraini: We've come a long way to be where we are today. And yet, when I observe how women are treated in very religious states in Malaysia, it's not going to be good, for women in general. The thing is, what worries me, they are the majority. It will affect the middle class first, because you must understand, a lot of the people in KL and Selangor, are not true KL/Selangor people – they came from other states. These people will be the change agents (for greater Islamization).

Rohana: When I hear that some women think they won't be affected by all this, it makes me think of the French aristocracy before the Revolution, living in blissful ignorance of what was to come.

Notwithstanding the concerns that these women feel about the consequences of increasing Islamization, neither they nor virtually anyone else in the Malaysian community is prepared to raise the issue in public. The reasons for this are complicated, and worthy of a separate academic study, but based on the feedback from the wider group of my participants, plus extensive literature research, they broadly consist of:

- a feeling of not being sufficiently expert in Islamic matters to question the conventional wisdom concerning interpretation, as articulated by the *ulama*;
- a fear of being out of step with Malay society, and the criticism and even ostracization that may follow;
- a fear of losing the privileges that go with being a senior member of the Malay community;
- a fear that the government could charge them with an offence such as 'insulting Islam', or 'sedition' (at the time of writing four members of the Opposition, and one academic, have been charged with sedition, in the previous month alone).

Illustrating the reality of this, Dina Zaman in her book, *I Am Muslim*, described a 2005 survey she helped conduct, in which educated Malays were interviewed regarding their perceptions of being a Muslim in Malaysia. She paraphrased their reaction as follows:

Yes, they're proud and happy that they are Muslims. Yet there were frustrations in being Muslim in Malaysia. How they want an Islamic country, but not in the way it is now. How little tolerance is shown not only to non-Muslims, but also to other Muslims. *We have issues that need to be aired, but we can't, because we could get into serious trouble, and with that lose our rice bowls'* (italics original). (Zaman 2007, 60)

One group that is an exception to the rule are the women of SIS, whose mission, as stated on their website, is: 'To promote the principles of gender equality, justice, freedom and dignity in Islam and empower women to be advocates for change' (http://www.sistersinislam.org.my/page.php?36). They attempt to educate the Malaysian Muslim public as to the way the Islamic texts should really be interpreted, rather than in the manner articulated by the *ulama*, who in SIS's view have a Traditionalist, patriarchal bias. They argue that:

> Malaysians have in effect delegated total and absolute responsibility for the interpretation of Islam to a tiny, often authoritarian, minority whose views and values are often contrary to the vision of Islam held by some federal leaders and by the silent majority of Malaysians. (Othman 2005, 95)

They see the Islamization advances to date as the thin edge of the wedge, with the end game quite possibly an Islamic state, a logical consequence of which is likely to be that women's rights will be seriously eroded, as is the case with other such societies elsewhere in the world.

## Conclusion

The qualitative data gathered for the project suggests that of the 20 Malay women interviewed, most were concerned about Islamization and its impact on their private and public life. They also shared concern about the fact that they believe the Islamization trend will continue, and apprehension about what it may lead to. Though the small size of the sample suggests its limited applicability to the totality of Malay women, it does point to concerns emerging among the elite, or the professional classes, about the trajectory of Islamization in Malaysia.

## Disclosure statement

No potential conflict of interest was reported by the author.

## References

Ahmed, Leila. 1992. *Women and Gender in Islam*. New Haven, CT: Yale University Press.
Alatas, Syed Hussein. 1977. *The Myth of the Lazy Native*. London: Frank Cass.
Andaya, Barbara Wilson, and Leonard Y. Andaya. 1982. *A History of Malaysia*. London: Macmillan.
Anwar, Zainah. 1987. *Islamic Revivalism in Malaysia: Dakwah among the Students*. Petaling Jaya: Pelanduk.
Anwar, Zainah. 2001. "What Islam, Whose Islam? Sisters in Islam and the Struggle for Women's Rights." In *The Politics of Multiculturalism: Pluralism and Citizenship in Malaysia, Singapore and Indonesia*, edited by R. W. Hefner, 227–252. Honolulu: University of Hawai'i Press.
Anwar, Zainah. 2008. "Advocacy for Reform in Islamic Family Law: The Experience of Sisters in Islam." In *The Islamic Marriage Contract: Case Studies in Islamic Family Law*, edited by Asifa Quraishi and Frank E. Vogel, 275–284. Cambridge, MA: Harvard Law School.

Barr, Michael D. 2010. "The Islamisation of Malaysia: Religious Nationalism in the Service of Ethnonationalism." *Australian Journal of International Affairs* 64 (3): 293–311. doi:10.1080/10357711003736469.

Djamour, J. 1959. *Malay Kinship and Marriage in Singapore*. London: Athlone Press.

Firth, R. 1966. *Housekeeping among Malay Peasants*. New York: Humanities Press.

Frith, Tabitha. 2001. *Reflexive Islam: The Rationalisation and Re-enchantment of Religious Identity in Malaysia*. Melbourne: School of Political and Social Inquiry, Monash University.

Hassan, Riaz. 2008. *Inside Muslim Minds*. Melbourne: Melbourne University.

Hooker, M. B. 1976. *Adat Laws in Modern Malaya: Land Tenure, Traditional Government and Religion*. Kuala Lumpur: Oxford University Press.

Horowitz, D. L. 1994. "The Qur'an and the Common Law: Islamic Law Reform and the Theory of Legal Change." *American Journal of Comparative Law* 42 (2): 543–580.

Jomo K. S. 2004. "The New Economic Policy and Interethnic Relations in Malaysia." *Identities, Conflict and Cohesion Programme*, Paper 7. Geneva: United Nations Research Institute for Social Development

Kabeer, N. 1988. "Subordination and Struggle: Women in Bangladesh." *New Left Review* 168: 95–121.

Kessler, Clive S. 1992. "Archaism and Modernity: Contemporary Malay Political Culture." In *Fragmented Vision: Culture and Politics in Contemporary Malaysia*, edited by Joel S. Kahn and Francis Loh Kok Wah, 133–157. Sydney: Allen & Unwin.

Kessler, Clive. 2014. "Where Malaysia Stands Today." *Malaysia Today*, May 14. Accessed January 29, 2016. http://www.malaysia-today.net/where-malaysia-stands-today/.

Liow, Joseph. 2003. "Deconstructing Political Islam in Malaysia: UMNO's Response to PAS' Religio-Political Dialectic." *RSIS Working Papers 45*. Singapore: Institute of Defence and Strategic Studies. Accessed January 29, 2016. http://www.isn.ethz.ch/Digital-Library/Publications/Detail/?lang = en&id = 27021.

Malaysian Department of Statistics. 2010. "Population Distribution and Basic Demographic Characteristics Report 2010." Accessed January 29, 2016. https://www.statistics.gov.my/index.php?r = column/ctheme&menu_id = L0pheU43NWJwRWVSZklWdzQ4TlhUUT09&bul_id = MDMxdHZjWTk1SjFzTzNkRXYzcVZjdz09.

Martinez, Patricia A. 2000. "From Discourse to Dissent? Theorizing the Construction of Women in Postcolonial Islam: Malaysia." PhD diss., Temple University.

Ministry of Women. 2014. *Study to Support the Development of National Policies and Programmes to Increase and Retain the Participation of Women in the Malaysian Labour Force*. Kuala Lumpur: Ministry of Women, Family and Community Development.

Mohamad, Maznah. 2009. "Paradoxes of State Islamization in Malaysia: Routinization of Religious Charisma and the Secularization of the Syariah." *Asia Research Institute Working Paper 129*. Singapore: National University of Singapore.

Mohamad, Maznah. 2014. "Women, Family and Syariah in Malaysia." In *Misplaced Democracy: Malaysian Politics and People*, edited by Sophie Lemière, 175–191. Kuala Lumpur: Strategic Information and Research Centre.

Nagata, Judith. 1980. "Religious, Ideological and Social Change: The Islamic Revival in Malaysia." *Pacific Affairs* 53 (3): 405–439.

Nagata, Judith A. 1984. *The Reflowering of Malaysian Islam: Modern Religious Radicals and Their Roots*. Vancouver: University of British Columbia Press.

Nair, Shanti. 1997. "Islam in Malay Politics." In *Islam in Malaysian Foreign Policy*, 14–54. London: Routledge.

Noor, Farish. 2000. "The Caliphate: Coming Soon to a Country near You?" Accessed January 29, 2016. https://www.hitpages.com/doc/4781550314979328/1#pageTop.

Noriani Nik Badli Shah, Nik. 2008. "Legislative Provisions and Judicial Mechanisms for the Enforcement and Termination of the Islamic Marriage Contract in Malaysia." In *The Islamic Marriage Contract: Case Studies in Islamic Family Law*, edited by Asifa Quraishi and Frank E. Vogel, 183–199. Cambridge, MA: Harvard Law School.

Oba, A. A. 2002. "Islamic Law as Customary Law: The Changing Perspective in Nigeria." *International and Comparative Law Quarterly* 51 (4): 817–850.

Ong, Aihwa. 1990. "State versus Islam: Malay Families, Women's Bodies, and the Body Politic in Malaysia." *American Ethnologist* 17 (2): 258–276.

Othman, Norani. 2004. "Islamization and Modernization in Malaysia." In *Women, Ethnicity and Nationalism: The Politics of Transition*, edited by Robert E. Miller and Rick Wilford, 170–192. New York: Taylor and Francis.

Othman, Norani, ed. 2005. *Muslim Women, and the Challenge of Islamic Extremism*. Petaling Jaya: Sisters in Islam.

Peletz, M. G. 2002. *Islamic Modern: Religious Courts and Cultural Politics in Malaysia*. Princeton, NJ: Princeton University Press.

Rahim, Lily Zubaidah. 2006. "Representing and Misrepresenting Islam: The Discursive Struggle between Literal and Liberal Islam in Southeast Asia." *APSNet Policy Forum*, February 9. Accessed January 29, 2016. http://nautilus.org/apsnet/0602a-rahim-html/.

Rajaendram, R. 2014. "More Female Enrolment at Tertiary Institutions." *The Sunday Star*, November 9. Accessed January 29, 2016. http://www.thestar.com.my/news/education/2014/11/09/more-female-enrolment-at-tertiary-institutions/.

Shaheed, Farida. 2004. "Constructing Identities: Culture, Women's Agency, and the Muslim World." *Women Living under Muslim Laws, Dossier 26*. Accessed January 29, 2016. http://www.wluml.org/node/478.

Shamsul, Abu Bakar. 2001. "A History of an Identity, an Identity of a History." *Journal of Southeast Asian Studies* 32 (3): 355–366.

Swift, M. 1963. "Men and Women in Malay Society." In *Women in the New Asia*, edited by B. Ward, 268–286. Paris: UNESCO.

Wain, Barry. 2009. *Malaysian Maverick: Mahathir Mohamad in Turbulant Times*. London: Macmillan.

Yeger, M. 1979. *Islam and Islamic Institutions in British Malaya: Policies and Implementation*. Jerusalem: Magnus Press and Hebrew University.

Zaman, Dina. 2007. *I Am Muslim*. Kuala Lumpur: Silverfish.

Zeitzen, Miriam. 2001. "Polygamy in Urban Malaysia: Gender, Islam and the Production of Elites." PhD diss., University of Cambridge.

Zeitzen, Miriam Koktvedgaard. 2008. "Muslim Polygyny in Malaysia." In *Polygamy: A Cross-Cultural Analysis*, 69–88. New York: Berg.

# Negotiating Modernity: Women Workers, Islam and Urban Trajectory in Indonesia

Nicolaas Warouw

**ABSTRACT**

The resurgence of Islam in its variety of practices has been one of the most important factors in defining contemporary Indonesian society. However, some have argued that it is only in recent decades that Islam has entered the public sphere of the nation with the largest Muslim population on Earth and affected the lives of people from many different walks of life. Economic development and globalization have provided Indonesia with a path towards industrialization in which rural subjects are transformed into urban industrial labourers. This shift has equally impacted on the way urban workers with a cultural background in the countryside perceive their devotion to Islam and represent their Islamic expression. This article focuses on the engagement of young female workers in company-sponsored Islamic gatherings (*pengajian*), which the participants have used to foster their own narratives both as daughters of rural Indonesia and as urban workers. I argue that the rural-urban transition and the subjects' incorporation of capitalist discipline contribute to the understanding of industrial workers' participation in, or, mobilization to, such gatherings in industrial towns. This article is based on fieldwork undertaken in Tangerang, a district to the west of Jakarta, in 2000 and 2001.

## Introduction

The resurgence of Islam in its variety activities – religious, cultural, economic and political – has been one of the salient defining points in contemporary Indonesian society. However, some have argued that it is only in recent decades that Islam has entered the public sphere of the nation with the largest Muslim population on earth and affected the lives of people from many different walks of life. Interest in Islam in Indonesia has also increased following the 9/11 attacks in 2001 in the USA, and the increase in religious tensions and violence in Indonesia allegedly related to the rise of Islamic fundamentalism, particularly after the fall of the authoritarian regime in 1998 (Barton 2004; Feillard, Madinier, and Wong 2011; Vicziany and Wright-Neville 2005). Apart from scholarly studies on religious fundamentalism, some have made attempts to understand Islam in Indonesia by focusing on its theological aspects, organizational forms (Barton 2002; Hamayotsu 2011), historical features (van Dijk 1981; Ricklefs 2006) and political significance (Kunkler and Stepan 2013; Porter 2002; Pringle 2010, 2011). In addition, Islamic expressions are similarly emergent in the everyday life of Indonesian society through marriage practices (Nurmila 2009), gender relations (Robinson 2008), moralities (Brenner 2011) and lifestyle (Smith-Hefner 2007). Furthermore, a number of studies have situated the practice of Islam within the practical context of the country's economic growth and globalizing economy (for example, Bahramitash 2002; Rudnyckyj 2008; Sakai 2010).

While most of these studies have been centred around contemporary urban, often middle-class, subjects, little attention has been paid to Islamic expressions embraced by working-class subjects employed in light manufacturing shop-floor activities that have characterized Indonesia's integration into the global economy and the world's consumer culture. Rudnyckyj (2008, 86–87), for example, has focused on the corporate-initiated inculcation of 'Islamic ethics' through training, in a steel factory in western Java at the beginning of the twentieth century to help establish 'in-built control' enabling employees to develop into 'self-governing, entrepreneurial subjects'. He views this form of 'spiritual reform', which could be read as 'critiques of materialism', as conditioning the employees not to question working conditions and material gains, but rather to focus on merging the religious ethics of individuality and accountability with capitalism to enable the company to be globally competitive. Earlier, within the context of the early decades of Indonesia's export-oriented industrialization, Mather (1985) addressed a contrasting reality in the strongly Islamic and conservative area of Tangerang, in the province of Banten, western Java, where industrial actions during the late 1970s were rare, despite the fact that factory women from local villages were paid half the wage received by those in neighbouring Jakarta. This apparent docility was related to the exposure of factory women, considered to be dependants in the Islamic worldview, to the patriarchal values adhered to by local Islamic institutions. Local figures, who were males from respectable families or Islamic personalities, Mather continues, acted as intermediaries between the employers and the workforce, and between factories and their surrounding communities (see also Warouw 2006). While Rudnyckyj's notion of Islamic ethics is somewhat in line with Max Weber's 'Protestant ethics', which laid a foundation for the rise of capitalism in nineteenth-century Europe, Mather saw Islamic values, especially patriarchal norms, being applied in society by industrial corporations as a means of control over female workers. Both Rudnyckyj and Mather confirm that Islamic expression might arise among industrial workers, too, in response to their exposure either to local culture or to global economic competition.

While confirming that the modern industrial sector was not immune to the flux of Islamic revivalism in the cultural sphere, both studies overlook the significance of the conditions of the rural–urban shift that characterize the existence of most industrial workers in Indonesia's urban centres. The recent development of the country's urban industries, dating back to former President Suharto's policies to attract foreign investment in manufacturing sectors since the early 1970s, and the inadequacy of the labour force for urban industrialization, have created conditions for the increasing presence of urban workers from rural backgrounds. These are young people who were born in the countryside, migrated to urban centres, and became the first generation in their rural family to engage in the urban industrial sector. The rural–urban spatial transition (or circulation) and the subjects' fresh incorporation of capitalist discipline are factors in industrial workers' religious expression.

This article discusses the participation of young female workers in their late teens in a religious gathering, the *pengajian*, in relation to their search for complete expression of modernity in their urban trajectory. Some informants whose comments are cited here seek to interpret acts of religious devotion practised by women workers who find them-selves in a larger context of rural–urban migration in relation to their becoming modern subjects. All informants are migrants from rural areas of Indonesia to Java, where they are employed in light manufacturing industries. The article begins with accounts of the changing face of the countryside as perceived by the informants, followed by the workers' experience of working in sweatshops and living in conditions of destitu-tion in a poor neighbourhood, their involvement in religious gatherings, and the contex-tualization of the situation through discussion of their status as both rural and urban subjects. It is based on fieldwork in Tangerang, an industrial town west of Jakarta, in 2000 and 2001, during the early years of the post-authoritarian era that followed the downfall of Suharto in 1998. The legacy of Suharto's 30-year regime nevertheless creates a background to accounts given in this article with regard to the changes in rural Indonesia and urban industrialization.

## The countryside

The decline of agricultural employment in the countryside has long been seen as the setting for the attraction of increasing numbers of rural youth to urban centres. However, assumptions about the 'structural failure' of agrarian development and the inca-pacity of rural employment to absorb new workers (Booth 1999, 137) seem to overlook the importance of economic development and changes in the countryside, especially since Suharto's rise to power in the late 1960s, in making a move to the city appealing to rural youth.

During the decades following Suharto's rise to power, the countryside has undergone what Young (1994) terms 'the urbanisation of the rural', in which rural areas are experi-encing major changes by adopting features previously regarded as urban-specific. In terms of material development, the image of an underdeveloped countryside has been replaced by the establishment of public and social infrastructure. A picture taken in 2000 at the Idul Fitri, a festival to celebrate the end of Ramadan, shows Ery, a female worker, with her parents and three siblings in the family home in a subdistrict town in Central Java. The house has brick walls and a plaster floor. According to Ery, the house used to be a wooden structure with a dirt floor but was renovated in the second half of the 1990s. Her father was a clove farmer who had benefitted from the improved market price of cloves following the collapse of the monopoly of the country's sole clove distributing and buying agency, which was associated with Suharto's youngest son.

Access to electricity has also changed rural society. Rural electrification means greater access to modern technology for most people in the countryside. The intensification of rural electrification has brought considerable change to everyday life. Electronic goods and appliances have become essentials. The first close encounter with television for most young migrants in the Tangerang industrial area was during their adolescent years in the countryside. The presence of television in their homes has encouraged more rural people, particularly the younger and more educated generation, to take up television-watching on a regular basis (see also Antlov 1999). The diversification of broadcasting channels has given rural people more choice of television shows and the variety of programmes offered by the private channels includes a significant proportion of imported material (Sen and Hill 2000, 121–122). Their exposure to these more vibrant programmes also exposes them to liberal ideas and the potential for change, as well as to foreign content and themes of modernity, which contribute to their ability to establish their place in the contemporary world.

In a home in a village in Central Java, where electricity only arrived in 1991, Ning and her younger sister, Dewi, as their recollections revealed, spent much of their time at home watching television after school in the afternoon and before going to bed late in the evening. The attraction of the private channels for these teenage girls, who are currently employed in a garment factory, was locally-made packages such as music, soap operas and entertainment news, which they continued watching even after they moved to Tangerang. The domestication of the television set has painted an urban face on the countryside and, accordingly, created an increasing distance between the rural youth and their agricultural surroundings. More time is spent in front of the television set and leisure time in the village is increasing as young people are reluctant to help their parents work in the rice fields. For the younger generation, television programmes and other forms of mass media have established urban life, the urban lifestyle and consumerism as their life's obsession and facilitated the creation of their future project to build a modern identity.

A 19-year-old urban worker in a furniture factory described days in a village in a western Java's subdistrict as being mostly occupied by non-farming activities. Before electricity came to the village and television ownership became widespread in the early 1990s, long hours were spent in outdoor activities, hanging out with peers. In the evening, children spent their time at Qur'an recitation (*ngaji*) in the mosque until about nine o'clock. Once television was present in the house, children were attracted to the locally-produced soap operas (*sinetron*) depicting young people's lives in metropolitan areas. As these serials were broadcast during prime time, children often snuck out of the mosque early in order not to miss their favourite television shows.

Apart from television viewing, school occupies a substantial number of hours in the everyday life of the younger generation in the countryside. The increase in formal education has uprooted rural youth from farm work. These days, a substantial portion of daylight hours are spent at school, from the age of seven (the minimum age requirement for primary education) to the completion of high school education at around the age of 18. Nine years of compulsory education has expanded school-aged children's mobility, as they travel on a daily basis to the nearest town or village where they can attend junior secondary school or even senior high school.

Through school, youth in the countryside learn about their imagined community of the modern Indonesia nation, a social projection in line with the state's design for material development. Textbooks provided by the state education authority have similarly introduced ideas of material and economic development (*pembangunan*). Leigh (1999, 44) argues that in Suharto's Indonesia '[t]he act of schooling' was part of human development as it represented 'a necessary rite of passage which integrates the person into the nation-state'. The introduction to ideas of development has, in turn, imposed a burden on rural children in the form of a self-image as part of the backwardness of the countryside. It is no coincidence that the discourse of development in many school textbooks captures images of asphalted roads, skyscrapers, a well-arranged city and airplanes, as well as a factory and its smokestack, symbolizing industrialization. This portrayal of material infrastructure, intended to deliver a vivid picture of progress to the students, implies a well-orchestrated effort on the part of the state to bring the ideas of development down to earth. This leads students to learn that conformity to the discourse of development is crucial for one to become modern.

One textbook, for example, had symbols of material wealth that an ideal family might afford, including fancy furniture, a television, radio, and car or motorbike. These provide an antithesis to rural underdevelopment, symbolized by the image of families with many children, bamboo houses with dirt floors, and unhealthy surroundings. As the 'process of exchange of ideas' in Indonesian classrooms is minimal, a textbook becomes an essential source to connect students to the knowledge taught by the teacher (Siegel 1986, 141–142). Parker (1993, 10) asserts that it is not only the students who have 'great reliance' on the textbooks, but also the teachers. This makes textbooks 'the sole source of information' for both the students and the teachers. The centrality of textbooks in Indonesian schools makes up what Leigh (1999, 35) calls '[t]ext as [a]uthority'; the truth is to be found in a 'black-and-white approach' from which the answer to every question in school exams at all levels of education can be found. There is no room for debate. Therefore, the recurring images appearing in the textbooks to which students are exposed at various levels of education at school mould the perception that progress is associated with order. They promote a particular form of modern life and being modern, which later affects children's perception of their future existence.

Although there is a primary school in almost every village, junior high schools serve students from a number of villages, while senior high schools are commonly located in the subdistrict town. Travel to a nearby town for education exposes rural youth to the experience of commuting on a daily basis. Travelling to school gives them a sense of independence in terms of mobility within a confined rural domain. This localized mobility, in turn, presents the youth with an opportunity to rehearse their future migration beyond local boundaries to metropolitan centres. As a result, future migration for non-educational purposes does not appear to be problematic for either parents or children, even girls.

A rural town offers villagers access to urban features that break rural isolation and undermines the myth about the backwardness of the countryside. Komala, a woman worker in the sanitary pad factory in Tangerang, told me that her first pop magazine was bought with savings from the pocket money given to her by her parents, when she was studying at a senior high school in a subdistrict town in West Java. After school, she frequently dropped in at a newsagent to get a particular magazine or tabloid that covered national as well as global pop stars she knew from television shows. Her favourite magazine was *Aneka*, a Jakarta-published pop magazine that covered entertainment news about popular icons and contained short stories about the romantic life of urban youth. She also collected posters and stickers in the magazine to display on the wall of her bedroom. This went on even after she moved to the urban neighbourhood in Tangerang. Now that Komala is an urban worker, her allowance from her parents is no longer necessary as she earns money from factory work. I have shown elsewhere that workers in Tangerang, like Komala, Dewi and Ery, spend their factory earnings mostly on consumer goods to sustain their perceived urban lifestyle in their urban neighbourhood rather than sending remittances home to the countryside (see Warouw 2004).

Exposure to education, media and popular culture means that forms of material culture that may initially have been thought of as urban have been introduced to rural youth through their encounters with ideas of modernity that have penetrated deeply into the Indonesian countryside. Marybeth Mills, in her study of Thai migrant workers (1999a, 5), found that rural children's obsession with urban 'progress and modernity' and 'glamor[ous] urban life and livelihood' has kept the urban labour market flooded with youth. This material and hedonistic attraction to the metropolis seems paramount in the minds and perception of rural youth, and generates what Harvey (1985, 251) terms a 'fetishistic reading' of urban phenomena. One informant, for example, stated that 'working in the village was hard (*keras*), frustrating (*kesel*), and exhausting (*capek*)'. At the same time, the confession continues: 'It looks like people in the city don't work as hard as us here in the village.' Young villagers began to understand the complexities of modernity, although still only partially, through mediated communication. They became more and more captivated by the idea of a successful happy family and the great results a hard worker, but still not working as 'hard' as in a village, can achieve.

Modern transformation in the countryside provides the younger generation with a point of reference for the way they foresee their future, which is not what their parents wish. Some parents were keen to send their children to study and live at the nearby Islamic boarding school, *pesantren*, so that they would be exposed to religious teaching. An informant's father, for example, wanted his child to learn about Islam as well as to have improved skills in Arabic and Qur'an reading. In addition, especially under Suharto as described by Headley (2004, 50), a proper education in Islam would also enable one to serve as a religious teacher at primary and secondary school and, hence, to receive a monthly salary. Headley, speaking on the situation of Islam in central Java, therefore maintains that knowledge of religion brings those who have it 'financial gain' and ultimately 'a rising social status'. This pragmatic view of religious practice is coherent with the laidback character of Islam in Javanese countryside, whereby Islam is taken in its 'synthesis' with the older Javanese values of the seventeenth century (516).[1] It is no coincidence that *slametan*, a ritual communal feast in Javanese peasant tradition as presented by Geertz (1960, chs 1–7),[2] was one of terms used by urban workers recollecting their childhood days in the countryside. The above-mentioned informant left the *pesantren* after just over one year, apologized to his parents, and told them that the call of the city was more appealing.

The rural youth's pursuit of being 'modern', which leads to urban migration, is often linked to the local expression *tidak ketinggalan jaman* (not being left behind by the changing epoch). This resonates with Ferguson's (1999) notion about urban migration in Zambia being a catalyst for villagers to fulfil their expectations about freedom and pleasure. It also parallels Mills' (1999a, 5) observation about Bangkok factory workers, that the drive for 'being up-to-date' highlights rural youth's enthusiasm for urban migration and urban cultural practices. There is a belief among rural children in Indonesia that one's life is not complete without 'going to town'. The search for a 'complete' identity by 'going to town' has inevitably expanded the geographical locality of rural people.

## The shop floor[3]

Urban factory work provides rural youth with different experiences and conditions from those of the rural setting in which they grew up. A factory shares characteristics of a 'total institution' in Goffman's (1971) sense, in which individuals are detached from the wider society and their previous existence and subsequently placed in circumstances where discipline and organization are designed to sustain the regime of industrial production. The incorporation into the industrial institution is marked by symbolic rituals imposed by the corporate agency, which strip off the identity and individuality of young workers. For Foucault (1991, 155), this enables the authority to create subordinate individuals as objects of power, as 'docile bodies' whose initiative has been subtracted and replaced by 'new forms of knowledge'. Thus, this incorporation is also the way rural children are introduced to the 'new mechanisms of power' that regulate their mind and body to conform to the corporate project of commodity production.

The internalization of such mechanisms is accomplished through habituating the self to capitalist production (Braverman 1974). The significance of habituation is not merely related to the technological transformation, but equally to the conditioning of workers to become an extension of machinery. This includes training workers to value the precision of task execution measured by the clock in order to ensure progression along the assembly line (see Thompson 1967). The transition to capitalist production therefore results in rural subjects organizing everyday life in accordance with clock-based time partition. A factory also offers workers industrial disciplines that meticulously define the individual's every movement in order to achieve maximum efficiency in achieving the objective of capitalist production. The implementation of these disciplines requires surveillance machinery, which, along with time-based organization and habituation to the routine operation, makes up what Foucault (1991, 221) terms 'the calculated technology of subjection' to replace the 'traditional … violent forms of power'. In labour-intensive corporations, the deployment of a surveillance mechanism is imperative to ensure that control from the highest echelons remains intact at the bottom level of the hierarchy.

The noise of machines, the sight of a factory's smokestack issuing forth thick, dark smoke, and the heavy container trucks all symbolize the grandeur of industrialization. There is the factory gate, through which the workers sign up for one domain and leave the other, and vice versa. Lining up in front of the gate is a morning ritual for all workers before they are allowed to enter the factory premises. They have to put on their identity badge, which is checked by the company's security officials. Failure to abide by the rule may affect the worker's future contract with the employer. The identity badge has become a vital attribute that can determine the very existence of an individual in an industrial setting, as dismissal and promotion are very much dependent on compliance with such rules.

The industrial factory can be seen to have attributes of the total institution. The badge is more than just an identity card for administrative and security reasons. It represents the programming of the worker's behaviour to conform to the industrial mindset and obligations. The badge, which has to be worn at all times in the workplace, represents the employee's commitment within the factory domain to abide by workplace regulations. If they do not display it, workers are unlikely to be considered as the company's responsibility and so there is a threat that their basic rights as employees will be ignored.

The accomplishment of the process of programming is also determined by management efforts to undermine the subject's identity. Within the institution, the principle of uniformity applies to every single subordinate individual and personal image relies on the definition generated by the authority. Stripping away attributes that have an association with the subject's prior existence is necessary. Personal attributes are the representation of self-identification, which may be in contradiction with the purpose of the institutions. This is illustrated in the case of Ery, a female migrant worker employed at a South Korean-owned footwear factory, which put in place a policy of body-searching before workers entered the plant. In this export-oriented company producing semi-casual leather shoes, workers are not allowed to bring food or drink from outside into the factory compound. Only food and drink provided by the company can be consumed in the designated canteen area during the set meal time. A few other articles are also subject to such exclusion. A white veil to cover the body and head for Islamic prayer (*mukena*) is not permitted on the shop floor, and is only to be used in the prayer room (*mushalla*) within the factory compound.

When interviewed, Ery said that she had become accustomed to such restrictions and could understand the underlying reasons. Having food and drink during work, as she said, might be a distraction from the production process. At the same time, however, she also claimed that it was hard to maintain physical well-being with only one break for a meal in an eight-hour-long shift when the type of work demanded concentration and physical labour. The spectacle of employees being scrutinized by the security guard is repeated at the end of a shift or overtime. They wait for their turn to be searched, including a body-search, before they can pass through the gate. At this end-of-shift search, the company's interest is in preventing the illegal removal of anything from the premises.

As in many other manufacturing companies in Tangerang, life in this footwear factory begins when the morning bell rings. At 7:30 sharp, the beginning of the shift, Ery – one of about 1000 workers employed in the plant – has to be sitting in her line in the hand-sewing area. Here, shoes are finished by hand-stitching a design on the plain shoe. Hand-sewing is the third stage in the overall production process. The normal work hours are until 3:30 in the afternoon, but workers in the hand-sewing division often do not return home until 10:30 or 11:00 in the evening. Ery explained that in the peak season, when demand for the products was high, the company forced the shop-floor employees to work overtime in order to meet production deadlines. The length of compulsory overtime varied from one division to another. During high season, divisions other than hand-sewing would complete their work as early as 6 pm or 9 pm. According to Ery, the use of machines made the work in other divisions more efficient and allowed shorter work hours. In contrast, work in the hand-sewing division was rather complicated. The manual nature of the work, in which the involvement of mechanical auxiliary tools was almost zero, made the task in the division the hardest of all production stages. Given this complexity, the company employed more workers, all females, in this section than in any other division in the company – nearly a third of the work force on the production floor. Though most workers acknowledged that the adjustment to corporate discipline was always difficult, given the pressure of work to meet production deadlines, they accepted the company's compulsory overtime policy. This acceptance was mostly pragmatic; they expected overtime to boost their earnings so that they could be more flexible in spending and could allocate expenditure to needs beyond daily basic necessities.

Break times were considered not frequent enough and too short for workers to recover after physical hard work that demanded total concentration during work hours. From morning bell at 7:30, they were only permitted to leave the production premises for one hour at 11:30 am for lunch and afternoon prayer. As food and drink from outside were not allowed, lunch was provided in the canteen by the company, and drinking water was available on the production floor. Tea was provided on the production floor on Tuesday and Friday only. There was no chance to relax during the break as all the workers had to line up to get their meals. Most Muslim workers went to the prayer room, located at the back of the complex, for Islamic prayer. Workers had to pick up what they needed for prayer at the front gate and then walk about 400 metres to the *mushalla* at the back, to fulfil their religious obligation. There might be a few minutes left, not enough for them to catch their breath, before they resumed working at 12:30 in the afternoon. If they were working overtime, they did not take a break at 3:30 in the afternoon in the transition between shifts. The afternoon shift break for dinner and prayer was even shorter, from 6 pm to 6:30 pm. Lining up for one's meal, eating, walking to the *mushalla*, and prayer, all had to be done in half an hour. After dinner, there would be no break until the end of the shift.

Conditions in the production building were blisteringly hot, partly because the outside temperature might reach 32°C during the dry season. In addition, many complained that the building's asbestos ceiling caused high temperatures in the poorly ventilated workplace: 'The asbestos is right over our head, no wonder it is so hot inside.' Several fans were installed but were unable to cool the room to prevent the workers from sweating. The working environment became more unpleasant when the air resounded with the deafening noise that came from the blower machine drying the adhesive used in the assembling division. When asked whether the noise disturbed their physical well-being and concentration, a teenage worker responded: 'I'm already used to that noise, I'm not troubled anymore.' Most employees in the company had become accustomed to the repugnant and hazardous nature of the work. They had to be extra careful in dealing with particular materials and substances in their area. The dust that came from the leather had the potential to cause skin irritation. Workers in the moulding division were at risk of exposure to the chemical substance used to soak the leather. Hand-sewing workers, particularly when they were tired, were vulnerable to accidents caused by the sizeable and unhygienic needles that might wound a finger, leading to swelling that could last for several days.

In the manner of a total institution, a factory has all the means – from fortress-like walls, badges and body-searches, to control apparatus – to contain workers in a reality different from that outside the factory barrier. It concentrates a large number of men and women in more or less similar activities, geared towards commodity production in capitalist enterprises. Apart from the relentless work, which tests human endurance, values brought from past existence, mostly gained in the countryside, can also become a benchmark by which rural youth can judge the unjust practices and degrading treatment within the factory regime. A comparison of life in the village with life in the factory, as well as the perception of the benevolent countryside, are potent sources of ideological critique of the degraded working conditions in urban manufacturing firms. Despite offering a steady and increasingly improving income, the factory shop floor remains an alienating reality for rural youth. This suggests that, despite the discipline the total institution imposes on the workers, the incorporation of rural youth into capitalist production is never complete.

## Young women, factory work and a *pengajian*

Around five minutes before 5 pm, Nur hurriedly tidied up her work station, removing leather pieces and work tools from around a sewing machine where she had been working since 7 am. Her work station, along with hundreds of other sewing machines, was part of a production line at a leather shoe factory located in Tangerang. That afternoon, she had completed the daily production output of leather shoes specified by her immediate supervisor. A little earlier, a shop-floor assistant carrying a trolley had collected piles of shoes from each work station, counted them, and put every detail on record. Luckily for Nur, none of her shoes was rejected for failing to pass quality control. Otherwise, she would have had to stay longer to redo the work.

At 5 pm, when an alarm echoed throughout the South-Korean-owned factory, Nur, along with other girls in their late teens, rushed impatiently but quietly to the main gate to leave the premises. They had to pass a security check by uniformed male guards to ensure that no company property was being illegally taken out by employees. In work hours, except during a half-hour lunch break, the company rules forbade shop-floor workers to talk, even to workmates sitting beside them. Only workers' verbal responses and enquiries related to instructions given by the line supervisor were allowed. Once they were out of the factory, located in one of the Tangerang industrial estates, chatter was heard from the girls walking home through an asphalted street with a factory brick wall on both sides. They joined the throng of workers from other companies who were also finishing their shift.

After about half a kilometre, the street became a dusty clay lane as the industrial landscape switched to densely populated urban residential quarters (*kampung*) typically inhabited by low- to lower-middle income earners. Nur and the other girls continued walking to the interior of the quarter, passing houses, rows of lodgings, and the hurly burly of the human crowds in the neighbourhood. Two stopped by at street-side vendor's to buy cooking ingredients, while others waited. Shortly after, they arrived at a place where they had lived since their arrival in the town a year or two earlier. They called it *mes* (dormitory). There were six barrack-like rows in the dormitory, which was hired from a local landlord by the company that employed the girls, who were mostly from the Javanese countryside. The *mes* was part of a large residential compound also comprising other rows rented out by the landlord to individual workers arriving from rural towns and villages in Java, Sumatra, and as far as Sumbawa island in eastern Indonesia and employed in surrounding industrial estates.

At the dormitory, the girls had hardly any time to relax after an almost eight-hour shift plus two hours' overtime. A long queue of compound residents waited their turn to get water from the well and another long line formed outside the shared bathrooms and lavatories, while others washed clothes by hand, and some squatted next to a kerosene stove on the floor to prepare the evening meals. These were some of the late-afternoon scenes in this workers' compound.

For Nur and her workmates, the bustle, including dinner, had to conclude a few minutes after 7 pm, when the local mosque delivered the call to *isha*, the evening prayer. That day, workers from Nur's company were dismissed early to enable them to prepare to attend the regular *kelompok pengajian*, a Qur'an recitation group, held fortnightly on Wednesdays at the dormitory. On any other normal workdays, when the demand for production was high, shop-floor employees at Nur's factory had to work overtime until early or even late evening. The exception for that Wednesday was possible because the *pengajian* was sponsored by the employer. The company allowed it to be held at the dormitory, provided financial support for refreshments, lent a sound system and paid an honorarium to the speaker giving the religious talk.

The *pengajian* was attended mostly by girls like Nur, who made up the majority of the workforce in this footwear corporation. They wore short-sleeved shirts or t-shirts, and pantaloons or jeans, their everyday casual outfits, especially when off duty. The only difference was that they covered their hair with a simple headscarf as was customary for women when attending Islamic religious activities. At least 70 people were sitting cross-legged face-to-face in two long rows on the tiled floor on the terrace of the dormitory. Only five of them were males but their presence was crucial. After a female host uttered a *Basmala* (in the name of God, the Most Gracious, the Most Merciful), gave the *Assalam alaykum* (peace be upon you) greeting, welcomed the gathering, and read out the programme for the evening, she handed the microphone she had been using to a man beside her.

A man with a moustache in his late twenties or older, who looked more mature than others that evening, received the microphone, thanked the host, repeated the earlier greetings, and gave an introductory speech. The man, known as Mas Joko, was a foreman of the company and assigned to be the head of the company's dormitory (*kepala mes*). It was presumably for his well-built dark-skinned posture that the company gave him this responsibility; he helped the residents and ensured their well-being, and gave protection to the country girls in this urban setting whenever necessary. On other occasions, most female occupants confirmed that this was true. In his short speech that evening, he reiterated the message that the *mes* residents, the employees and the employers were altogether part of a big family (*keluarga besar*) whose members had to lend a hand to each other. Shortly after, he handed back the microphone to the host, who thanked Mas Joko and invited another man to take his turn.

This man, who was probably the same age as Mas Joko, was called *ustadz*, an honorific accorded to a man who had superior knowledge of Islam, and had been requested, as the host said, to give a sermon (*ceramah*) that evening. The *ustadz* began by reciting Islamic prayers in Arabic, concluding with *Sūrat al-Fātiha*, a verse from Qur'an, uttered jointly with the audience. He then continued by speaking about balancing work and religious life and about *pengajian* being the way to strengthen the faith (*menguatkan iman*) so that one would not fall into the temptation of committing wrong. He frequently added Arabic verses from the Qur'an to emphasize his points. At other times, he contextualized his speech with stories from Hadith, which made him the authority of the gathering that night. The way *pengajian* progressed that evening was very familiar for my informants, who treated it as an equivalent of the *slametan* ritual they had known since their childhood in the countryside. The only difference, they said, was in the *ustadz* who led the ritual.

The *ustadz* was also an employee in the same footwear company. However, unlike Nur, her colleagues and Mas Joko, who were on the production floor, the *ustadz* was in the administration office, often referred as being part of *manajemen* (management), and was therefore regarded by the workers as being higher in the work hierarchy. He knew in detail the work environment and conditions on the shop floor, which became the setting of his sermon. Despite the strict, elaborate discipline and bureaucratic procedures imposed by manufacturing corporations on shop floors, a softer approach was also often adopted by most companies in the area ensure workers' loyalty. This not only aimed at lightening the everyday experience of workers on the assembly line, but was also an attempt by the company to demonstrate its generosity towards employees and to create the image of a benevolent employer, concerned about workers' welfare. These measures ranged from the provision of sports facilities and space for prayer to sponsoring recreational trips and religious events, all of which were intended to 'accommodate the advancement of talent and creativity of the workers', as stated in Nur's company's work agreements (PTMKS 2000, 54). However, as workers at Nur's workplace almost unanimously agreed, the company's acts of generosity would not necessarily lead workers to have a sense of loyalty or emotional attachment to their employer. As the event ended and people began to leave the venue, Mas Joko was seen to surreptitiously pass to the *ustadz* a white envelope, probably containing the honorarium, when they were shaking hands.

## Reconciling rural home and capitalist discipline

Although there was certainly a spiritual atmosphere that evening, brought about by the prayers and Qur'an recitation, and the participants seemed to solemnly follow the proceedings and pay careful attention to the *ustadz*'s speech, the presence of the girls, nevertheless, reveals more about their existence as factory workers and rural 'daughters'[4] than it does about their religious adherence to Islam. For them, the *pengajian* reveals a reality that is more than just religious.

Female workers like Nur were reluctant to have to work up to 10:30 in the evening, spending 15 uninterrupted hours on the production floor, with only short breaks for mealtimes and prayers. Prolonged work hours, as they said, gave them little chance to do other things for leisure and domestic tasks at home. Nur's workmate from the same assembly line said:

> Working until that late means we don't have enough time to take a night rest, because on the following day we have to be in the factory again at 7.30 in the morning. Working until 8.30 in the evening would be quite enough (*pas-pasan*). When we get home, there would still be time to wash our clothes, do something else, and we can get enough rest.

For most workers who had to keep working after normal work hours, having to stay in the plant until late evening brought a feeling of discomfort. This was not only because the evening was supposed to be a time of peaceful respite: many admitted that it felt strange to have to work hard after dark. She continued:

> In the village I could hear the call to prayer from the mosque (*azan*) almost all the time. Early in the morning I could hear people reading Qur'an (*ngaji*). Those practices reminded me not to put work to earn a living before spirituality.

This indicates her acceptance of workplace discipline but with reservations resulting from an extension of the experience migrants brought from their villages.

As also confirmed by informants from Islamic family backgrounds interviewed during my fieldwork, Ery remembered that most work activities to earn a living in her village ceased at dusk or when the air resounded with the early evening (*maghrib*) call to prayer from the mosque. For her, having to work for a living after dark indicated that she had compromised her spirituality for the pursuit of money (*mata duitan*). Referring to herself in the first person plural, she went on to say: 'It is like we don't have a God' (*Kita seperti nggak punya Tuhan*). Her statement was unusual, given that atheism in contemporary Indonesia continues to be seen as politically incorrect and subversive, since it is regarded as being parallel to Communism, which has been prohibited since Suharto's rise to power in the late 1960s. But, her remark about the seeming 'lack' of spirituality is related more to pre-conceived values related to 'subsistence ethics' (Scott 1976) that she believed to be innate in rural people like herself, but absent in her urban existence as a factory worker. James Scott in *The Moral Economy of the Peasant* (1976) speaks of subsistence ethics as a mechanism practised in rural Southeast Asia to ensure food security among poor peasants and to keep them away from an agricultural catastrophe that would threaten their livelihoods. Thus, working overtime in the urban factory is likely to be regarded by a worker like Ery as performing labour that is beyond the level needed for subsistence and, therefore, violating the moral economy. The sense of disregarding this value is revealed in a self-critical confession she made about skipping prayers many times in exchange for, in her own word, 'money' (*cari uang*) during time on the shop floor. Although it has become common for a prayer room to be available in manufacturing workplaces, praying during production time was rather incompatible with the daily production target set by the employer for individual workers. 'Too much hassle, too much running around', said Nur, describing the effort needed to walk between her production line and the prayer room within her large factory compound.

In developing countries, rural values in the form of 'pre-existing images', as among Thai urban workers (Mills 1999b, 187), or 'images of the peasant', as found among the Venezuelan urban proletariat (Roseberry 1994), have been crucial to the development of the perspective of marginalized urban subjects on their existence in the city. Making a judgment of problematical conditions of subsistence in the city as compared with idealized practices in the countryside therefore provides grounds for 'a moral economy of protest' against urban scarcity (Roseberry 1994; see also Ong 1987). In Tangerang factories, taking part in a religious gathering like *pengajian* provided a medium for the girls to ease the tension that emerged in their negotiation with the industrial regime. 'No matter how busy I am in the factory, [attending *pengajian*] is the least I could do, that I still have God in my mind (*masih ingat Tuhan*)', said Nur. Meanwhile, Ery saw her presence in the gathering not just as an obligation she should fulfil as a Muslim, but also as something that assuaged her sense of guilt about working so hard to earn a living. 'It's not right to think about work and money all the time, is it?', she added. Their statements indicated that *pengajian* was more related to, and situated within, the context of their urban livelihood and engagement in factory work, which both girls saw as being problematic. At the same time, they were aware that the search for 'money' in their urban existence was also inevitable on their adventurous journey to become modern subjects in the city. This has made *pengajian* a means for workers to connect with the rural community by using romanticized pictures of the village to judge the appropriateness (or the lack thereof) of urban reality. *Pengajian* reveals the urban migrants' search for a way to make the countryside and its values present in order to give them peace of mind within their present existence as urban residents and factory workers.

## Idealizing the rural past

The event of that evening may also represent a non-religious ritual that enables its participants to maintain their ties with countryside. Many urban migrants perceive the countryside as a starting point for their migrating ventures, drawn by centrifugal force to urban centres. However, their young age and the uncertainty in their current employment as factory workers mean that their future remains unsettled, given the urban difficulties they have encountered. The annual return to the countryside for Idul Fitri festivities, during which the affinity with their place of origin is constantly reinforced, is indicative of the unbroken ties that exist between the countryside and its departing children. Returning home and paying their respects to the kinship group is a pilgrimage in which Idul Fitri returnees seek blessings and good wishes from the elders as a source of spiritual strength to help them gain success in their future enterprises. While Idul Fitri is an annual event, participation in *pengajian* on a fortnightly basis constantly maintains ties with the rural home.

Developments in Javanese villages whose population has changed from farmers to urban migrants do not necessarily lead villagers to relinquish their 'village identity', as Headley (2004, 191) puts it. Urban migrants from a rural background were aware that the countryside remained a place of refuge from the hurly burly of the cities and the hardship of urban life. Some portrayed the city as being 'a place of evil' and danger whence all wicked deeds emanate and where one's destiny could never be envisaged. In contrast, rural home is regarded as a place where spiritual strength is generated. Others described the sound of the city, coming from stereo, radio or machinery at the factory, as having overpowered the call to prayer from nearby mosques, which often reminded them of the countryside, remembered as a quiet place with which the current city life had nothing to compare. All these confessions were made despite modern changes in rural areas as described earlier, which they also acknowledged.

Amid their efforts to conform to their modern identity, the very same subjects revealed that their cultural identification was more with the countryside than with their present existence in the city. It is probably for this reason that Nur, for example, chose to pay the annual *zakat* (alms-giving) in her home village rather than in the city where she had spent most of her time and income during the year. 'After all, my village remains a home for me and some benefits from my work [in the city] should go to the people at home too', she said, making a point about her connection with the countryside.

In contrast, *kampung*, their urban neighbourhood, is a domain where migrant workers experienced the partitioning of the city on the basis of economic categories, such that the affluent developed quarters are separated from the deprived underdeveloped areas. The destitute workers' lodgings, the shortage of basic facilities and the disorder, for example, generate a bleak picture of the dark side of industrialization. To female workers like Nur, Ery and many others, the neighbourhood where they made their home in the city was by no means a representation of the social status they hoped to attain on their urban journey. Sri, who is known to Nur and Ery but employed in a different factory, said that before her arrival in the city she had never dreamt of being stranded on the shop floor of a factory. On the contrary, 'I thought the city would have been pretty, much the same as the city I knew from *sinetron* (televised soap operas) where everything seemed easy and without many difficulties', admitted Sri. She mentioned a few *sinetron* serials that ostensibly presented the lifestyles of Jakarta's upper middle class, so it is no coincidence that Jakarta, the metropolis, is seen by her as the epitome of urban experience. It is a place in which, in the minds of the new arrivals, almost every sign of modernity matches the urban phantasmagoria induced by the mass media. 'All I knew was that Tangerang was no more than a suburb of Jakarta, so, to my knowledge, Tangerang itself was [identical to] Jakarta', explained Sri.

Their great expectations of exciting experiences and imagined urban life in the metropolis ended in immense disappointment and total disbelief when they got off the bus that had brought them from the countryside and stepped onto Tangerang ground. Rather, they felt the opposite: distress at the bewildering face of modernity and the harmful excesses of urban industrialization. High humidity, heavy air pollution from industry and motor vehicles, disorder in urban development, and chaotic traffic gave the girls a gloomy image of the supposed city. The deprived conditions of an industrial town were certainly a shock to them.

Therefore, being separated by hundreds of kilometres from their place of origin, urban migrants sought to bring the idea of home into their present existence to give them a temporary peaceful respite from urban hardship and, probably, from disappointment. Nur, for example, found that her dormitory was the place where she could find a sense of 'family' that reminded her being in a rural home. Most residents in the company's dormitory came from the same district, or subdistrict, if not the same village, as she. More importantly, she, Ery, Sri and other girls felt that they were sharing similar experiences: being away from home, encountering industrial disciplines for the first time in their life, and having to endure urban hardship. 'In this *mes,* I feel like I find a family', she said. She added, 'We have each other to laugh together and to cry together.' For migrants like her, maintaining rural-based relations was crucial to ease the alienating effect of industrialization and urban marginalization.[5]

*Pengajian* was consequently perceived by them within this context. Here is what Nur said:

> It is not merely about religiosity. It is a practice that we frequently had at home or in a local mosque in the village. The praying, the Qur'an recitation, and the sermon were all the same. *Pengajian* just reminds me of home, my childhood with parents. Coming to a gathering like this, but without my family, I feel like I could cry. [But] luckily I have other girls I have mostly known for long, or who come from the same district as me. It helps to cheer me up and be strong again.

She also said that these experiences were all she was longing for from the evening *pengajian* held regularly in the company's dormitory. In addition, Sri added that the gathering was when the girls were able to meet in a relaxed atmosphere in a setting outside the workplace. She continued, 'Although we often see each other, on any other day we are too exhausted from work and don't care too much for each other. It [*pengajian*] is like a reunion (*kangen-kangenan*).' It is probably no coincidence that residents of this dormitory generally describe each other, or even other workers in the neighbourhood, as being part of a 'family'. The term is likely to refer to an extension of social forms and encounters that originated from familial relations and other close-knit ties typically found in rural communities.

The religious gathering these female workers were attending and in which they were emotionally engaged does not only signify an appropriation of religious symbols (the ritual and its attributes) and observance of religious obligations. It was a practice in which Nur, Sri, Ery and many other workers addressed their situations. A practice that had appeared to be ostensibly religious turned out also to be a non-religious compassionate tale about their early exposure to modern cultural discourse, their expectations of modernity, and their conflicting experience in becoming urban subjects. At the same time, it maintained their association with their rural identity. *Pengajian* symbolizes an attempt to reconcile these encounters: to keep migrants on track in their quest to become modern subjects, but then again to remain true to the Islamic values they considered to be mediating their connection with the rural past.

## Concluding remarks

The urban migrant workers' search for modernity is a negotiation between, on the one hand, perceived social imaginings of modernization and modernity established during their rural existence and, on the other, their contemporary urban presence. As the actual urban experience contradicts such imaginings, a reconciliatory action such as taking part in religious gathering is required to mediate these paradoxes.

The *kampung* has been the ongoing subject of constant marginality. The participation of female workers presented in this article is not by any means the only way in which the subjects negotiate with urban social antagonism typical of a capitalist society in industrializing countries. This is made possible by making present the idea of a relatively happier less-troubled past at the very centre of their urban existence. Engagement in *pengajian* represents the workers' aspiration to make sense of all the contrasts in the urban reality and find the audacity to cope with their sustained presence in the city. Appadurai (1996, 192), speaking of conditions in conflict-torn regions, points out that, even in rather extreme and transitional circumstances, displaced people, or refugees, managed to create a 'neighbourhood' where they were able to live a normal life and perform rituals as in relatively less-troubled circumstances. In Tangerang, *pengajian* reveals a process, rather than an event, of incorporating the urban landscape into their domain of home – once provided only by the rural home areas – and duplicating some rural forms of life in the conditions of the new home in the city. It enabled young girls like Nur, Ery and their colleagues to develop customs and practices that had previously belonged to the rural home.

Years later, I returned for two short visits to the area in 2008 and 2009. The town and the neighbourhood remained the same, but were more crowded. None of the female informants cited in this article were still in the dormitory. They had either married and moved to other neighbourhoods across the town or got other jobs with different companies. Some other former informants, however, indicated that they had not given up their urban life and career as factory workers. Those who had married had decided to do so of their own free will. Their spouses are factory workers whom they had met in the city. Parental intervention in their personal life, let alone in terms of arranged marriage, is thus non-existent. This appears to be unlike Naafs' (2012, 59) recent discovery amongst the young women of Cilegon, a neighbouring rural town to the west of Tangerang. In a semi-rural setting, as Naafs indicates, young women who live with their parents are expected to abide by local custom, which requires them to get married and stop working once they reached adulthood. The role of cultural norms in women's choices is similarly observed in studies by Smith-Hefner (2005) and Nilan (2008) about chastity and acceptance of arranged marriage being chosen by young people as part of their dedication to Islam.

Amidst the spread of Islamic expression in Indonesian society as indicated in the studies referred to at the beginning of this article, Naafs (2013), however, argues that observing a permissive, consumer-based lifestyle in balance with religious morality remains possible in a traditionalist Islamic community undergoing neoliberal industrialization and increased consumerism. Nevertheless, religious belonging as practised by female workers in *pengajian* reveals more about their search to balance their identity between being daughters and workers than about their religious piety. With the present generation of migrants being more prepared to make their future life in an urban setting (Warouw 2004), while also adhering to the idea of being a good daughter, religious gathering and representation symbolically reminds the departing children of the community from which they came. While Islam remains as a nominally cultural identity, the changing environment following the rural–urban shift allows young female workers to have a relaxed outlook when it comes to expressing religious belief.

In my recent visit, it was not easy to breathe the air of the resurgence of Islam in public life. There were usually only a few female workers wearing headscarves wandering the streets in the neighbourhood, except when they were undertaking religious duties such as the five daily prayers or religious gatherings. Just like a decade ago, those who normally wore a headscarf in public were quite relaxed when, by chance, they met an outsider like me when their heads were uncovered. I rarely saw them rushing to grab their headscarf when non-relative males happened to appear. Urban hardship remains, but it does not interrupt the urban trajectory of women workers. They change jobs to work for different manufacturing employers. They move from one urban neighbourhood to another. Others find romance in the city. At the same time, the image of the rural home and of being daughters, and the allure of the countryside hover over their religious practices, through which they express their wish to continue to belong to the community into which they were born.

## Notes

1. In Indonesia's general social and political landscape, this position is associated with Nahdlatul Ulama, the country's largest Islamic organization with predominantly rural constituents.
2. The ritual is typically associated with a Javanese social category known as *abangan* (Geertz 1960), a term that is also often used in a wider contemporary context to refer to non-practising Muslims (Headley 2004, 26).
3. A significant portion of this section has been previously published in Warouw (2008).
4. Wolf (1992) introduced the term 'factory daughters' to refer to rural young workers employed in light manufacturing industries in Central Java's countryside being under obligation to contribute to the economy of their parents' households.
5. Elsewhere, Rebecca Elmhirst in her study of the northern Lampung (Sumatra) diaspora in Tangerang (2004) maintains that an 'ethnicised' urban social network serves the function of fostering emotional ties with migrants' home towns. It offers them a sense of security and social insurance amidst the insecure nature of Indonesia's light manufacturing sectors.

## Acknowledgements

I express many thanks to the informants whose views are included in this paper. The names are pseudonyms. This paper is initially based on a dissertation project at Department of Anthropology, Research School of Pacific and Asian Studies, The Australian National University between 2000 and 2004, during which I received an International Postgraduate Research Scholarship provided the Government of Australia and ANU scholarship. I would like to thank Kathryn Robinson, Andy Kipnis, Patrick Guinness and Ben Kerkvliet for their contribution in my panel of the thesis supervisory board. The current paper was prepared as a contribution to a 2013 Muslim Womanhood Seminar held at the University of New of South Wales (UNSW) at ADFA campus in Canberra as part of UNSW's Asia Pacific Seminar Series (APSS) project. Thanks to Professor Samina Yasmeen (UWA) and Dr Minako Sakai (UNSW), both of whom were convenors of the seminar, as well as the two anonymous reviewers who made insightful comments. Thanks also to Susan Cowan for her proofreading work on this article. The editorial assistant and copy-editor have also helped to put the article into its present form. All remaining errors are my own.

## Disclosure statement

No potential conflict of interest was reported by the author.

## References

Antlov, H. 1999. "The New Rich and Cultural Tensions in Rural Indonesia." In *Culture and Privilege in Capitalist Asia*, edited by M. Pinches, 188–207. London: Routledge.

Appadurai, A. 1996. *Modernity at Large: Cultural Dimensions of Globalization*. Minneapolis: University of Minnesota Press.

Bahramitash, R. 2002. "Islamic Fundamentalism and Women's Employment in Indonesia." *International Journal of Politics, Culture, and Society* 16 (2): 255–272.

Barton, G. 2002. *Abdurrahman Wahid – Muslim Democrat, Indonesian President: A View from the Inside*. Sydney: University of New South Wales Press.

Barton, G. 2004. *Indonesia's Struggle: Jemaah Islamiyah and the Soul of Islam*. Sydney: University of New South Wales Press.

Booth, A. 1999. "The Impact of the Crisis on Poverty and Equity." In *Economic Crisis: Origins, Lessons, and the Way Forward*, edited by H. W. Arndt, and H. Hill, 128–141. Singapore: Institute of Southeast Asian Studies.

Braverman, H. 1974. *Labor and Monopoly Capital: The Degradation of Work in the Twentieth Century*. New York: Monthly Review Press.

Brenner, S. 2011. "Private Moralities in the Public Sphere: Democratization, Islam, and Gender in Indonesia." *American Anthropologist* 113 (3): 478–490.

Elmhirst, R. 2004. "Labour Politics in Migrant Communities: Ethnicity and Women's Activism in Tangerang, Indonesia." In *Labour in Southeast Asia: Local Processes in a Globalised World*, edited by R. Elmhirst, and R. Saptari, 387–406. London: RoutledgeCurzon and International Institute of Social History.

Feillard, A., R. Madinier, and W. Wong. 2011. *The End of Innocence? Indonesian Islam and the Temptation of Radicalism*. Honolulu: University of Hawaii Press.

Ferguson, J. 1999. *Expectations of Modernity: Myths and Meanings of Urban Life on the Zambian Copperbelt*. Berkeley: University of California Press.

Foucault, M. 1991. *Discipline and Punish: The Birth of the Prison*. London: Penguin.

Geertz, C. 1960. *The Religion of Java*. London: Free Press of Glencoe.

Goffman, E. 1971. *Asylums: Essays on the Social Situation of Mental Patients and Other Inmates*. Harmondsworth: Penguin.

Hamayotsu, K. 2011. "The End of Political Islam: A Comparative Analysis of Religious Parties in the Muslim Democracy in Indonesia." *Journal of Current Southeast Asian Affairs* 30 (3): 133–159.

Harvey, D. 1985. *Consciousness and the Urban Experience: Studies in the History and Theory of Capitalist Urbanization*. Baltimore, MD: John Hopkins University Press.

Headley, S. C. 2004. *Durga's Mosque: Cosmology, Conversion and Community in Central Javanese Islam*. Singapore: Institute of Southeast Asian Studies.

Kunkler, M., and A. Stepan, eds. 2013. *Democracy and Islam in Indonesia*. New York: Columbia University Press.

Leigh, B. 1999. "Learning and Knowing Boundaries: Schooling in New Order Indonesia." *Sojourn: Journal of Social Issues in Southeast Asia* 14 (1): 34–56.

Mather, C. 1985. "Rather Than Make Trouble, It's Better Just to Leave: Behind the Lack of Industrial Strife in the Tangerang Region of West Java." In *Women, Work, and Ideology in the Third World*, edited by H. Afshar, 153–180. New York: Tavistock.

Mills, M. B. 1999a. *Thai Women in the Global Labor Force: Consuming Desires, Contested Selves*. New Brunswick, NJ: Rutgers University Press.

Mills, M. B. 1999b. "Enacting Solidarity: Unions and Migrant Youth in Thailand." *Critique of Anthropology* 19 (2): 175–192.

Naafs, S. 2012. "Navigating School to Work Transitions in an Indonesian Industrial Town: Young Women in Cilegon." *Asia Pacific Journal of Anthropology* 13 (1): 49–63.

Naafs, S. 2013. "Youth, Gender, and the Workplace: Shifting Opportunities and Aspirations in an Indonesian Industrial Town." *Annals of the American Academy of Political and Social Science* 646: 233–250.

Nilan, P. 2008. "Youth Transitions to Urban, Middle-Class Marriage in Indonesia: Faith, Family and Finances." *Journal of Youth Studies* 11 (1): 65–82.

Nurmila, N. 2009. *Women, Islam and Everyday Life: Renegotiating Polygamy in Indonesia*. Hoboken: Taylor and Francis.

Ong, A. 1987. *Spirits of Resistance and Capitalist Discipline: Factory Women in Malaysia*. Albany: State University of New York Press.

Parker, L. 1993. *Gender and School in Bali*. Canberra: Gender Relations Project, Research School of Pacific Studies, Australian National University.

Porter, D. J. 2002. *Managing Politics and Islam in Indonesia*. London: RoutledgeCurzon.

Pringle, R. 2010. *Understanding Islam in Indonesia: Politics and Diversity*. Honolulu: University of Hawaii Press.

Pringle, R. 2011. "Indonesia's Moment: It Is the World's Most Populous Muslim-Majority Nation and a Highly Successful Democracy. How Did Indonesia Do It?" *Wilson Quarterly* 35 (1): 26–33.

PTMKS. 2000. *Kesepakatan Kerja Bersama* [Enterprise Bargaining Booklet]. Tangerang: MKS Pty Ltd – SPTSK.

Ricklefs, M. C. 2006. *Mystic Synthesis in Java: A History of Islamization from the Fourteenth to the Early Nineteenth Centuries*. Norwalk, CT: Eastbridge.

Robinson, K. 2008. *Gender, Islam and Democracy in Indonesia*. Hoboken: Taylor and Francis.

Roseberry, W. 1994. *Anthropologies and Histories: Essays in Culture, History, and Political Economy*. New Brunswick, NJ: Rutgers University Press.

Rudnyckyj, D. 2008. "Worshipping Work: Producing Commodity Producers in Contemporary Indonesia." In *Taking Southeast Asia to Market: Commodities, Nature, and People in the Neoliberal Age*, edited by J. Nevins, and N. L Peluso, 73–87. Ithaca, NY: Cornell University Press.

Sakai, M. 2010. "Growing Together in Partnership: Women's Views of the Business Practices of an Islamic Savings and Credit Cooperative (Baitul Maal Wat Tamwil) in Central Java, Indonesia." *Women's Studies International Forum* 33 (4): 412–421.

Scott, J. C. 1976. *The Moral Economy of the Peasant: Rebellion and Subsistence in Southeast Asia*. New Haven, CT: Yale University Press.

Sen, K., and D. T. Hill. 2000. *Media, Culture, and Politics in Indonesia*. Melbourne: Oxford University Press.

Siegel, J. T. 1986. *Solo in the New Order: Language and Hierarchy in an Indonesian City*. Princeton, NJ: Princeton University Press.

Smith-Hefner, N. 2005. "The New Muslim Romance: Changing Patterns of Courtship and Marriage among Educated Javanese Youth." *Journal of Southeast Asian Studies* 36 (3): 441–459.

Smith-Hefner, N. 2007. "Javanese Women and the Veil in Post-Soeharto Indonesia." *Journal of Asian Studies* 66 (2): 389–420.

Thompson, E. P. 1967. "Time, Work-Discipline, and Industrial Capitalism." *Past and Present* 38 (December): 56–97.

Van Dijk, K. 1981. *Rebellion under the Banner of Islam: The Darul Islam in Indonesia*. The Hague: Nijhoff.

Vicziany, M., and D. P. Wright-Neville. 2005. *Terrorism and Islam in Indonesia: Myths and Realities*. Clayton: Monash University Press.

Warouw, J. N. 2004. "Assuming Modernity: Migrant Industrial Workers in Tangerang, Indonesia." PhD diss., Australian National University.

Warouw, N. 2006. "Community-Based Agencies as the Entrepreneurs' Instruments of Control in Post-Soeharto's Indonesia." *Asia Pacific Business Review* 12 (2): 193–207.

Warouw, N. 2008. "Industrial Workers in Transition: Women's Experiences of Factory Work in Tangerang." In *Women and Work in Indonesia*, edited by M. Ford, and L. Parker, 104–119. London: Routledge.

Wolf, D. 1992. *Factory Daughters: Gender, Household Dynamics, and Rural Industrialization in Java*. Berkeley: University of California Press.

Young, K. 1994. "A New Political Context: The Urbanisation of the Rural." In *Democracy in Indonesia: 1950s and 1990s*, edited by D. Bourchier, and J. Legge, 248–257. Clayton: Centre of Southeast Asian Studies, Monash University.

# Traditional, Islamic and National Law in the Experience of Indonesian Muslim Women[†]

Bernard Adeney-Risakotta

**ABSTRACT**

This article examines how social imaginaries of women as equal in the public sphere, rooted in a long history, support gender equality. However, there is tension between national law, traditional (*adat*) law and Islamic law in the narratives of Indonesian Muslim women. In Indonesia, law is not conceived of as a universal boundary that may not be violated, but rather as a discursive tradition subject to negotiation depending on local conditions. In some parts of Indonesia, women are imagined as powerful agents who have often exercised leadership in society. In other parts, patriarchy is strongly entrenched. Law, and the imaginary of women, is in an ongoing process of transformation in response to the dynamic between modern education, global religious influences and traditional practices. Traditional law is grounded in the narratives of people within specific local ethnic groups and interacts with Islam and changing modern conditions to create unique local understandings of the role of women in society. National law in Indonesia often has less authority than religious and traditional law. Both the interpretation of law and the prevalence of women in positions of leadership are supported by imaginaries of women as powerful actors in the public sphere.

## 1. Introduction

The largest Muslim population in the world lives in Indonesia. This land of 17,000 islands includes around 220 million Muslims, half of whom are women. Reid (2014a) has argued that, compared with Europe, Indonesia enjoys a longer history of relative gender equality. This is borne out by many current laws designed to empower women and protect their human rights. There are many progressive Indonesian Muslim women's organizations that are active in promoting the empowerment of women. On the other hand, Indonesian Muslim society also appears to be strongly patriarchal, with men holding most positions of power. How can we understand the paradox between the 'feminist' character of Indonesia and the 'patriarchal' nature of Indonesian Muslim society? Part of the explanation may lie in the reality of Indonesian legal pluralism. Indonesian women have to navigate laws

---

[†]This article stems from research done in connection with an Indonesian Consortium for Religious Studies research project on Religion and Public Policy in Southeast Asia, funded by the Henry Luce Foundation. The second year of the project focused on the influence of religion on public policy as it affects women. See also Adeney-Risakotta (forthcoming).

governing the relationships between women and men from three major traditions of law: national law, Islamic law and traditional (*adat*) law.

National law guarantees gender equality. Islamic law, which is authoritative for Muslims in the areas of marriage, family and inheritance, appears to favour male precedence. Meanwhile, traditional *adat* (ethnic, tribal law) varies widely across this great archipelago. Among Muslim majority ethnic groups, *adat* inheritance laws are sometimes bilineal, sometimes patrilineal and sometimes matrilineal. Some areas, such as Riau in Sumatra, include both matrilineal and patrilineal strands of law. To confuse things further, some groups, such as Muslim Javanese, have been termed 'matrifocal', meaning that the mother is the person who wields the most influence and authority in the family (Geertz 1961).

Two Muslim sisters in the Gayo highlands of Aceh, in Northern Sumatra, Indonesia, were given land by their mother, who had received the land from her father (their grandfather).[1] The women were born on the land and had built houses and worked the land for many years. Years later, an army officer came to the village and claimed that he was the rightful owner of the land. He was the cousin of the two sisters, the son of their mother's older brother. According to him, their common grandfather had only loaned the land to their mother and when he died, the land should have been inherited by this cousin's father, who was the grandfather's oldest son. Then, in turn, his oldest son (this army officer) had a right to inherit the land (see Figure 1) because, according to Gayo traditional law (*adat*), the oldest son inherits the land. This is reinforced by Islamic law (*fiqh*), which assigns male heirs double the inheritance of their sisters. National law favours gender equality in inheritance cases, but defers to the local inheritance laws of *adat* and to religion.

Traditional *adat* law recognizes gifts of land, so if the grandfather really did give the land to his daughter, his eldest son would not have any legal claim to it. Violating the authentic wishes of the patriarch (grandfather/ancestor) could have serious supernatural consequences for the whole community. The grandfather is a powerful ancestor who could bring sickness, disaster or death if his wishes and promise are set aside. Each party

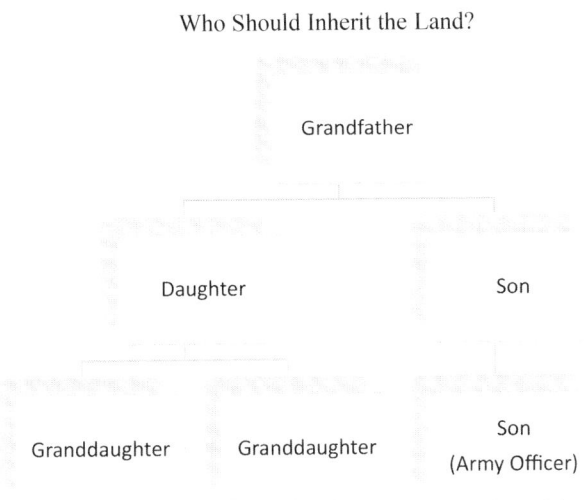

Figure 1. Who should inherit the land?

produced a land certificate and brought conflicting witnesses as to whether the land had been given to the patriarch's daughter as a gift or a loan. It was difficult to prove the competing claims.

The Islamic courts decided the case by negotiating between three different sources of legal authority: *adat*, Islam and the state. While the Islamic court was clearly sympathetic to the claims of the sisters, in the end the land reverted to the patrilineal line of inheritance. According to John Bowen, Gayo *adat* strongly favours inheritance through the male line that is native to the village. 'Sons and their families exert a greater control over resources than do daughters and their families and this inequality can be represented as sanctioned by *adat*' (Bowen 2003, 43). The decision was not the result of impersonal, deductive application of *adat*, Islamic law (*fiqh*) or national law, but rather of consideration of the relative merits, power and influence of parallel forms of legal discourse in the context of a patriarchal social imagination.

## 2. *Adat* tradition and Muslim women

For some Indonesian Muslims, the most binding and important legal structure is *adat* – the body of traditional stories, laws, regulations and practices of their ethnic group. *Adat* law is passed down from the ancestors and grounded in the ongoing story of the group. Violations of *adat* law bring immediate social repercussions, which may, at the extreme, include expulsion from the group. For many Indonesians, this is a fate worse than death. Violation of *adat* also risks supernatural sanctions brought on by God or the ancestors, such as sickness, disaster or death.

*Adat* law is intertwined with patriarchal social, economic and political structures, even in matrilineal societies. Some ethnic groups have a long history of subordination of women to men, while other groups are proud of traditions that empower women, including stories of women in positions of top cultural, religious and political leadership. For example, four queens (sultanas) ruled in Aceh consecutively from about 1640 to 1700. Among the 300 or so *adat* traditions, there are matrilineal and matrifocal societies where women exercise power and responsibility. However, most *adat* groups are patrilineal or bilineal and all are patriarchal.

Minangkabau culture in West Sumatra is famously matrilineal. Women own most property and pass it down to their daughters. However, men are still the leaders in political and religious affairs. The Minangkabau have produced some famously powerful women and are proud of their reputation for being fiercely committed to Islam. One such woman is Dewi Fortuna Anwar, who has this to say about the relation between Islamic law and matrilineal Minangkabau *adat*:

> Islam was put at the top, the highest body of law, to which the *adat* would be subordinated. The saying is: 'The *adat* would lean on the sharia and the *sharia* on the *Kitab*. (Scriptures)' ... Practices explicitly violating Islam were to be forbidden – drinking, gambling, cockfighting, marrying more than four wives. But other aspect are considered O.K., because there is nothing in the Koran or in the sayings of the Prophet against the matrilineal system. (Quoted in Naipaul 1998)

A Muslim Minangkabau woman in the History Department of Universitas Andalas (Padang) explained that, if a husband does not treat his wife well, she can just tell him to pack his bags and get out of the house, because women own all of the fixed property.[2] In Batu Sangkar, I asked the Head of the Council of Ulamas (MUI: Majelis Ulama Indonesia) how he reconciled Islamic *fiqh* laws on inheritance with Minang Kabau matrilineal *adat*. He explained that matrilineal *adat* law applies to all communal property (land, houses, furniture, etc.) that is passed down from generation to generation from mother to daughter. However, Islamic law applies to inheritance of personal property that is the result of a person's own private efforts in the public sphere.[3] This apparently neat solution is pregnant with many problems, since the private and public realms are not clearly separated in Indonesia.

Javanese *adat* follows bilineal inheritance laws, where wealth is inherited equally by men and women. But women often control the purse strings. Many Javanese men are expected to turn over all their earnings to their wife, who is responsible for managing household finances. An amusing example of this dynamic occurred when I gave a raise to our Javanese Muslim repairman and gardener. Pak Sungkana asked me not to give him a raise in his official salary, but only an equivalent 'bonus' every month. When I asked why, he explained that his wife took all his earnings and only gave him a tiny allowance for personal needs. If his salary remained the same, he would not have to tell his wife about the bonus and could have more for his personal needs. Of course he also asked me not to tell her about the bonus!

Javanese culture has been called matrifocal because the mother is the centre of responsible authority in the family (Geertz 1961; cf. Magnis-Suseno 1984). In the Javanese Muslim village where I live, social structures are clearly patriarchal, with men defined as heads of the family and holding all village leadership positions. However, many men are unemployed, while their wives work. The head of the village confirmed that the wives are the principle sources of income for most traditional Javanese Muslim households in the village, despite the fact that Islamic marriage law defines the husband as responsible for supporting his family. Since Javanese *adat* constructs women as more practical and 'earthy' than men, in a post-agrarian community the mothers go out and create work to feed and educate their families.[4] This gives men more time for religious activities, such as Qur'an recitation at the mosque, which brings God's blessing. Most mosque and other ritual activities are only attended by men. The exception to this rule is widows, who may attend village events as the head of their household. Some very old women pray frequently in the mosque, as they prepare for the next life.

Even without attending, women are involved behind the scenes in village rituals, cooking and blessing the ritual foods used. Smith (2008) argues that women play a vital role in *Kejawen*,[5] Muslim village rituals. They not only prepare the necessary food and offerings, but also play a key role in performing prayers and rituals behind the scenes, which ensures that there is a balance between male and female principles in the ritual. While this may be so in some Javanese villages, it remains true that 'public' positions of recognition and power are in the hands of men, while women remain leaders in the domestic sphere. As most Indonesians transition from family centred, agrarian, village economies to complex, urban economies where most of the functions traditionally carried out by the family are taken over by male dominated institutions, women may be further marginalized from communal authority (Adeney 1995).

## 3. Islamic law (*fiqh*)

Ninety-nine per cent of Indonesians claim that religion is important or very important to them personally.[6] Eighty-seven per cent of Indonesians are officially Muslim and many commentators have documented the increasing piety of Islamic practice in Indonesia (e.g. Ricklefs 2012).[7] For increasing numbers of Indonesians, *Syari'a* (Sharia) is the most important source of law. *Syari'a* is not the same as *fiqh* (Islamic law). *Syari'a* literally means 'the Way' (analogous to *Tao, Halakha, Logos* or *Dharma*). *Syari'a* is God's Law (with capital L), as it exists in the mind of God and is revealed in the Qur'an and *Sunna*. All Muslims are called to be obedient to the Law of God (*Syari'a*) in every area of life. In contrast, *fiqh* (Islamic law or jurisprudence) is the human interpretation of *Syari'a* and *Sunna*, expressed in positive laws and regulations governing everything from how to greet someone of the opposite sex, to what is a just punishment for stealing, to how you should purify yourself before prayer.

Some conservative Muslims deliberately elide *Syari'a* and *fiqh*. *Syari'a* is Divine Law and unchangeable. Therefore, to claim that a certain set of laws or regulations is *Syari'a* implies the claim that any attempt to change them is rebellion against the will of God. In contrast, *fiqh* is humanly constructed law that attempts to faithfully apply *Syari'a* to the conditions of a particular time and place. Hard-line, conservative Muslims equate early mediaeval formulations of *fiqh* with *Syari'a*. However, most Indonesian Muslim scholars distinguish *fiqh* from *Syari'a*, thereby legitimating changes in Islamic law to adapt to changing circumstances. To illustrate, a high percentage of Indonesian Muslims believe that Indonesian law should be based on *Syari'a*, which includes principles of justice, morality, human rights, care for the poor, forbidding murder and theft, etc. But only a small percentage believe that thieves should have their hands chopped off.[8] Hard-line conservatives claim that cutting off the hands of thieves is part of *Syari'a*, but most Indonesian Muslim scholars would say it is *fiqh*, Islamic law that was appropriate at one time, but is no longer relevant in a modern nation-state.

Islamic law (*fiqh*) is the area where religion and public policy have the most impact on women. Since the marriage law was passed in 1974 (Law 1, 1974 on Marriage) and the Religious Judicature Act was passed in 1989 (Law 7, 1989), the Religious Courts (*Pengadilan Agama*) have been granted broad powers and greatly increased resources for implementing *fiqh* for Muslims in the area of marriage and family law. *Fiqh* is construed as complementary to positive law, interpreting the marriage act of 1974 as it applies to Muslims. The interpretation of the marriage law for Muslims is governed by the Compilation of Islamic Law (*Kompilasi Hukum Islam*; CIL), which was issued by President Soeharto in 1991 as a Presidential Instruction. It is not a law, but rather 'a guide to applicable law for Judges within the jurisdiction of the Institutions of Religious Justice in solving the cases submitted to them'. (Elucidation, 5. Cited in Hooker 2003, 23). The intent of the CIL is to promote the very modern agenda of legal uniformity across all the Islamic courts in Indonesia. Prior to the CIL, Muslim judges were free to draw from diverse texts and schools of Islamic law to support their own interpretations of *fiqh*, but now the CIL supplies one set of guidelines for all the judges in the religious courts.

The CIL is more progressive on many points than traditional *fiqh*, which assumes an Arab patriarchal social structure from over a thousand years ago. Among many improvements, CIL limits child marriages, imposes heavy conditions for the permissibility of polygamy and gives wives improved rights within marriage and divorce. Nevertheless, the CIL is vigorously criticized by some Indonesian Muslims, both men and women, who argue that it conflicts with the Constitution and ratified international conventions. The Constitution guarantees gender equality before the law. In 2003, the Department of Religion appointed a team of Islamic law experts, led by Dr Siti Musdah Mulia, to produce a revision of the CIL in line with Muslim jurisprudence and the Constitutional mandate for gender equality. The committee produced a thorough revision, based on Islamic theological reasoning, called the Counter Legal Draft (CLD), which was released in 2004. The CLD caused such a storm of protest from conservatives and mainline Muslim organizations (including Nahdlatul Ulama and Muhammadiyah) that the Department of Religion withdrew the draft in 2005 before it was deliberated in the Legislature.

The CLD remains a major reference point for Indonesian women who want to reconstruct *fiqh* to be consistent with international protocols of human rights. However, the CIL is still the effective law of the land for Muslim family courts. Progressive Muslim women who wish to see the CIL reformed are opposed by Muslim legal activists who hope to see the CIL enforced as the law of the land. To the consternation of Muslim progressives, Muslim conservatives are currently lobbying for the CIL to be upgraded from a Presidential Instruction to a positive law.

One reason why the CIL is so hard to revise is that it encapsulates the social imaginaries of many Indonesian Muslims regarding the proper relationship between men and women. During his 32 years in power, former President Soeharto depoliticized everyone, but especially women. Much of the nationalist women's movement was wiped out with the purge of Communists. Most women's organizations were disbanded and the government supported only one woman's organization (*Dharma Wanita*), whose main agenda was to teach women to be good modern housewives, whose primary purpose in life is to support their husbands and care for their children. This social construction was presented as women's *kodrat* (natural law or essential nature). According to Soeharto, opposition to natural law risked shaking the foundations of society. Soeharto believed that an ordered family was also the foundation for economic development.

Even before the fall of Soeharto, bookstores in Indonesia became flooded with guidebooks (*panduan*) for women, most of which provide Islamic religious justification for women to dedicate their lives to pleasing God, their husbands and their children. I recently visited the largest general bookstore in Yogyakarta (Catholic owned) and found a huge section in the Religion area with books and pamphlets dedicated to Islamic guidebooks for women. I wondered why the guides are only addressed to women. Is there no need for such instruction for men? One book caught my eye that perhaps provided an answer. Its title (in Indonesian) was, 'Why the Majority of People in Hell Will be Women', with a subtitle 'How to Keep Women out of Hell'. Skimming through the book, I got the impression that most women would go to hell because they were weak and could not control their desires. Therefore, they found it difficult to fulfil their *kodrat* (natural law) of dedicating their whole life to God, their husbands and families. According to this line of thinking, to keep out of Hell, women need to obey and please their husbands more.

Books and pamphlets may be one of the least powerful sources of religious instruction that promotes an imaginary of women as domestic objects, created for the pleasure and service of men. Similar messages are projected through TV programmes, advertisements, movies, the Internet, computer games and social media sources. Fortunately, most Indonesian women do not accept a message of extreme subordination to men. Over the past 23 years, virtually all of my Indonesian women graduate students in Muslim, national and Christian universities have been committed to empowering women in all sectors of society. The vitality of hundreds of women's organizations, from the grass roots all the way up to the highest levels of government, points to a different social imaginary from that of the conservative religious media.

Public policy primarily impacts women through law. Unequal laws that discriminate against women are unlikely to be accepted by society if they violate dominant social imaginaries. Conversely, however, laws that are backed up by the resources of the state help shape the social imaginaries of the people. Currently, the *de facto* law of the land regarding women and families for about 220 million people in Indonesia is the CIL. The following is a brief analysis of some aspects of the law regarding marriage which, according to Dr Siti Masdah Mulia, enshrine a social imaginary of women as subordinate to men.[9]

(1) Marriage is defined as an act of worship in obedience to God's command. This implies that marriage may not require the agreement of the woman, since it is not defined as a covenant between a man and a woman, but rather as obedience to God's command. Also implied is that someone who does not marry may be in disobedience to God. A single woman cannot carry out this act of worship. By refusing to marry she may be rebelling against her *kodrat* (inherent essence) as a woman, created by God to bear children and serve her husband. Mulia suggests defining marriage as a covenant between two people.

(2) The Bride must have a male representative (*wali*). This implies that an adult woman cannot legally marry through her own agency. Rather, she belongs to a male who has the right to make major life decisions on her behalf. In contrast, an adult man does not need a representative because he has the right and power to enter into a marriage covenant by his own decision. The requirement that a woman must have a male *wali* in order to marry implies that she is not equal with men before the law. In fact, she is not an adult subject (whatever her age), with the power to represent herself and sign a legally binding marriage agreement.

(3) A marriage must have two male Muslim witnesses. This implies that women and non-Muslims are not competent to witness and legally legitimate a Muslim marriage. This suggests that women do not have individual autonomy before the law. Even if there were a thousand adult woman witnesses, the marriage would still not be legal without two Muslim male witnesses.

(4) The minimum age for marriage is 19 for the groom and 16 for the bride. Since brides cannot marry themselves or enter into a marriage covenant by their own decision, it does not matter if they are still children when they marry. Legally, the marriage agreement is made by their adult representative, not by the girl. In contrast, the man must be over 18 so that he is competent to sign the marriage covenant as an adult. The designation of 16 years as the minimum female marital age is an important advance over traditional *fiqh*, which does not list any minimum age. It may be influenced by modern human rights protocols on the protection of women and children.[10]

(5)   A marriage gift (*mahar*) must be paid by the groom to the bride. This may imply that the groom must pay a bridal gift (*mas kawin*) to have the woman transferred from subordination to her father to subordination to her husband. A Muslim woman professor argued that the mahar is a protection for the woman, since if she is mistreated and returns to her parents, the *mahar* (which may include valuable property) returns with her to her family. The bridal gift is not imagined as a payment to buy the bride, but rather as a sign of commitment and high honour given to the woman. Nonetheless, the legal requirement of a gift from the man to the woman is at best a sign of an imbalance in power between the man and the woman and at worst may feed the imaginary of a woman as being property that can be bought if you have enough money. In most traditional adat communities, marriage gifts flow both ways, with gifts from the groom to the bride and gifts from the bride to the groom. The value of the respective gifts may be more determined by the relative social status of the two families than by the gender of the giver (see Adeney-Risakotta 2005).

(6)   A legal marriage is one that fulfils the requirements of Islamic law. It should be registered with the state for administrative purposes. In Indonesia, many marriages are not registered with the state. They are still considered religiously legitimate marriages (*sah*) as long as they include a wali, two male witnesses and a bridal gift. However, this leaves the bride and her children with no legal protection in case of death, divorce or desertion. The state has no legal proof that the marriage took place. Since most of the legal rights associated with marriage are only available after the marriage is registered, it seems logical that a marriage should be registered before it can be declared legal. This issue is especially important in Indonesia, where there is a common practice of 'temporary marriages' (*mut'ah*) and 'customary marriages' (*sirri*), which are sometimes used to provide religious legitimation for prostitution and/or human trafficking. Tourists or business people sometimes contract for a religiously sanctioned 'temporary wife' during their trips to Indonesia (Mukhotib 2002).

(7)   A wife is required to be obedient and not rebel against the husband's orders or she may be declared *nusyuz* (not fulfilling her responsibilities as a wife). This implies that the wife is below the husband, rather than his partner. She is obliged by law to obey him, as long as he does not ask her to break Islamic law. This means she has no agency to oppose her husband according to her conscience. This clause includes serious negative legal and financial implications for the wife, in the case of divorce or marital conflict. The gender inequality of this clause is a problem, but so is the vague definition of 'obedience', 'rebellion' and 'responsibilities as a wife'. The husband enjoys unwarranted power to manipulate the nature of the marital problem in case of conflict. Musdah Mulia (2008, 62) suggests that the best way to overcome this problem is to legally require both husband and wife to be obedient to their responsibilities in the marriage.

(8)   The husband is the head of the family (*Kepala Keluarga*) and the wife is the mother of the household (*Ibu Rumah Tangga*). This implies that the state defines a relationship of subordination in the marriage, with the husband as leader, and assigns the wife primary responsibility for taking care of the house and family. Some women activists see this as the heart of the problem with the CIL, since it explicitly sets out a position of inequality between a man and a woman in marriage and before

the law. Many Muslim families experience harmony and equality, even though both spouses imagine the husband as the head of the family. That is up to the conscience of each family. However, women activists argue that, by stating subordination as part of the legal definition of marriage, the CIL does not allow for alternative imaginaries of marital relations.

(9)  The husband is the family breadwinner and responsible for taking care of his wife and family. This construction of the relation between husband and wife ignores modern reality. In many Indonesian families, the woman is the primary breadwinner and has more income than her husband. This clause suggests that men who are not the primary economic support of the family are somehow deficient. A positive implication is that during the birth and early years of his children, the husband is legally responsible for taking care of his wife and children. In the past, childbirth and childcare took up practically the whole of a woman's life. Now, because of birth control, longer lives, technology, health care, education and different economic structures, women can be free to work outside the home for most of their lives. This traditional social imaginary of the economic relation between husband and wife ignores the great changes in social and economic structures that characterize modern life.

(10)  Marriage to more than one wife is legal but limited to no more than four wives. Polygyny is only permitted if the husband can treat all of his wives and children justly. If a husband is unable to be fair to more than one wife, he may not marry more than one. This implies that polygyny is legal but polyandry is not. It is interesting that, of all the critical reactions to the CLD, by far the most emotional and vehement rejection was against the proposal to remove polygyny as a legitimate legal option for Muslims. None of the other proposals elicited such a heated response (Mulia 2007, 144). Less than 1% of marriages in Indonesia are polygamous and polygyny is disapproved of by most Indonesians of both sexes. When famous figures do marry more than one wife, they risk almost universal outrage and a radical loss of popularity, not to mention a high chance of divorce (Nurmila 2008). However since the Qur'an explicitly allows up to four wives, a marriage law that forbids polygyny is seen as un-Islamic. The CIL restricts polygamy by making it illegal for anyone who cannot be just to all of his wives. Some critics think that, if these restrictions were followed, polygyny would be practically illegal in the context of Indonesia.

(11)  A Muslim may not marry a non-Muslim. This implies that Muslim citizens and their families do not have the right to marry according to their conscience, if it crosses the line between religious communities. Ironically, this introduces a little gender justice over traditional fiqh, which permits Muslim men to marry non-Muslim women, but forbids Muslim women from marrying non-Muslim men. Perhaps this is a backhanded acknowledgement of the increasing autonomy of Muslim women in the modern world. The CLD allowed both men and women to marry non-Muslims, thereby provoking a strong reactions from religious conservatives. In Indonesia, inter-religious marriages occur quite commonly, in spite of legal difficulties. Social sanctions between the two families are usually more effective than national law in preventing inter-religious marriages.

(12)  If a marriage is dissolved by death or divorce, the woman (unless she is a virgin) must observe a period of abstinence (iddah) during which she may not remarry. This may be a wise policy for both parties. One reason for this waiting period is to determine

whether the woman is pregnant and who is the father. However, another reason is to give an opportunity for reconciliation to both parties before a divorce is finalized. This seems to be a good reason to make it required for both parties. Mulia argues that if it only applies to woman, it implies that a man does not need time for calm assessment whereas a woman does.

(13) If a marriage is dissolved by the death of the husband, the wife must observe a period of mourning (*ihdad*) for the same period as is determined for the *iddah*. If the marriage is dissolved by the death of the wife, the husband should observe a period of mourning as appropriate. This implies that there is no fixed period of mourning for the husband, but only for the wife. Does this imply that women are weaker and should be prevented from rashly remarrying after their husband dies, whereas the husband can remarry as soon as he feels it is appropriate?

(14) A child born out of wedlock only has a legal relationship to the mother and her family. Critics argue that this absolves men of all responsibility for children they create through sexual activity outside of marriage. If a man impregnates a woman, he and his family do not have any legal responsibility to support the child. Furthermore, the child has no rights of inheritance from the father or his family. This might encourage a social imaginary in which women are required to be sexually chaste, except within the bounds of marriage, whereas men are free to 'sow their wild oats'. In the past, the paternity of a child born out of wedlock was considered impossible to prove. However, in the modern era, proof of paternity is possible thought DNA testing. Muslim feminists argue that biological fathers should be held responsible for the children they produce.

The CIL includes a curious combination of traditional and modern concerns. It was compiled from *fiqh* during the Soeharto administration and framed to reproduce an ideology of family promoted by the government as the best basis for economic development. In keeping with the New Order passion for centralization, it sought to eliminate diversity and inconsistency in the practice of religious law. Religious law was harnessed for reproducing a patriarchal social structure and protecting the *status quo*.

Soeharto identified the leftist women's movement as powerful supporters of his arch enemies, the Communists. The New Order fabricated images of wild and free Communist women (*Gerwani*), sexually torturing distinguished generals, in order to arouse the Muslim community to wipe out Communism. The CIL produced an alternative imaginary of good Muslim women as innocent, submissive and pious. Women were construed as domestic subjects, obedient to God and their husbands and supportive of the gender ideology of the government's approved women's organization, the Dharma Wanita.

The CIL was created to serve a modern political agenda and has persisted unchanged for over 24 years because it was compiled by sincere Islamic scholars who believed it to be the best *fiqh* for the context of Indonesia in a rapidly changing world. The CIL clearly responds to some of the demands of Muslim feminists to strengthen the rights and position of women within marriage. But it also fulfils the desire of many conservative Muslim scholars to keep close to the verbal formulations about marriage in the Qur'an and *Sunna*. Mainstream Muslim scholars criticized the CLD because it 'exceeds the limits of reinterpretation or that it conflicts with accepted doctrine' (Mulia 2007, 143). According to some scholars, interpretation (*ijtihad*) is only permissible if something is not clear. Things that are clear in the Qur'an should be obeyed, not interpreted.

Unfortunately, what is clear or unclear is determined by one's social imaginaries. Even conservative Muslim scholars do not object to reinterpretations of *Syari'a* when they correspond with their imaginaries of ideal social reality in the modern world. For example, conservative Acehnese clerics see no need to include the *hudud* corporal punishments, such as cutting off the hands of thieves, in applying Islamic *Syari'a* in Aceh, even though they are literally (and clearly) commanded in the Qur'an.[11] Instead, they focus on *Syari'a* laws that control the dangerous power of female sexuality, even in areas that are not touched on in the Qur'an and *Sunna*. For example, in some parts of Aceh, women are required by *Syari'a* law to ride side-saddle on the back of motorcycles, rather than in the safer position astride the bike. Certainly, there are no literal Arabic instructions governing women on motorcycles in the Qur'an and *Sunna*. But this is considered an area legitimate for *ijtihad* (interpretation), since it is clearly unclear! What is clear is that some male clerics find women astride a motorcycle to be unacceptably erotic.

## 4. Imaginaries of Muslim women in Indonesia

Riaz Hassan has surveyed attitudes about women and society in several different Muslim majority countries (Indonesia, Pakistan, Egypt and Kazakhstan). Not unexpectedly, Indonesia scored by far the highest in terms of percentages of men (65%) and women (78%) who hold 'modern' views of the role of women in society (Hassan 2002, 180). For example, unlike in the other countries, most Indonesian men and women agree that women may: work outside the home, earn more than men, receive higher education and become leaders. Similarly, Indonesia scored significantly higher than other Muslim countries in the Gender Empowerment Index of the United Nations Human Development Report (Hassan 2002, 203), The Gender Empowerment Measure (GEM) calculates the relative empowerment of women in various aspects of public life and in comparison with men. Indonesia received the highest GEM score of any Muslim country.

It is apparent on even casual observation that Indonesian women are more active and visible in public life than, for example, in Pakistan. When I visited Islamabad and Rawalpindi in 1989, my impression was of cities with no women. Only 10% of the people in public spaces[12] were women, and all of them were veiled from head to foot in black chadors that covered the face. Some even covered their eyes in black gauze. Public transport was gender segregated and all the buyers and sellers in the market place were men. Most women seemed to be confined to their homes. The absence of women was startling to me, since I had just come from Indonesia, where women in brightly coloured clothing seemed to dominate public spaces.

Therefore, it came as a surprise that, according to Hassan's research, Indonesian men and women scored higher than other countries, including Pakistan, in agreeing that women should be veiled and segregated from men. The attitudes of Indonesian Muslim men and women were overwhelmingly (80%) in favour of women wearing Muslim dress and being separated from men. The measurement of this attitude was based on the percentage of men and women who agreed with the following sentence: 'Women are sexually attractive, and segregation and veiling are necessary for male protection'

(Hassan 2002, 195). Why do Indonesian women score so high on favouring women's equal participation in public life, while also agreeing with veiling and segregation?

Indonesian Muslims imagine 'veiling' and 'segregation' quite differently from Muslims in Pakistan and the Middle East. Veiling and segregation are voluntary in Indonesia and do not restrict women to the home or forbid their participation in public life. Many Indonesian women imagine Muslim dress and separation of the sexes as means of empowerment rather than as restrictions on their activities. Veiling may be imagined as a restriction on men's right to look, rather than a restriction on what women wear. It is not a sign of submission but rather of men's weakness. Muslim dress serves as a protection from male harassment.

Most Indonesian men and women agree that women are beautiful, sexually powerful and attractive. The dangerous power of women is the subject of many myths, ghost stories and soap operas. In popular films, most ghosts are portrayed as beautiful women who lure men to their death. Many Indonesian men would readily agree that they need protection from the dangerous sexual power of women. The danger of beautiful women is part of their attraction.

Head coverings have a long history in many of the traditional cultures of Indonesia, irrespective of religion. They are part of flamboyant local styles that serve a variety of practical purposes in a tropical climate. Distinctively Muslim dress for women is a more recent trend, whose meaning keeps evolving. It is rare to see a woman wearing a long black chador. Most women wear colourful headscarves (*jilbab*) in an expanding repertoire of attractive styles. The so-called veil does not cover the face and is often coupled with the latest fashion styles. One of my students used the phrase 'jilbab Britney Spears' to designate the common practice of students wearing head coverings along with tight and sexy clothing. *Jilbabs* have changed not only in fashion, but also in their political meaning. At one time, they were a sign of opposition to the Soeharto government. They also serve as markers of pride in Muslim identity and resistance to Western domination of fashion. Protecting men from temptation may be one of the reasons why women wear a head covering; it is probably not the dominant reason (Rachmah 2008; Doorn-Harder 2006; Hooker 2003).

For hundreds of years, most traditional and religious practices in Indonesia have separated the sexes. In village meetings, worship in the mosque, socialization at parties, ritual meals, chanting of the Qur'an and work in the fields, women and men tend to group together with others of their own sex. Many children go to Islamic schools (*pesantren*) where boys and girls are separated. In some Indonesian churches, the men sit on one side and the women sit on the other. Similarly, Balinese Hindu women and men perform different functions in the temple. Separation of the sexes is customary and habitual in everyday life.

Hassan's research suggests that most Indonesian men (68%) and women (70%) believe that men should be the head of their families and that women need men's leadership (Hassan 2002, 201). *Surprisingly,* approval of 'patriarchy' among Indonesians appears much higher than among Pakistani men (62%) and women (44%). Statistics can lie and survey questions may lead people astray. However, it is interesting that 70% of Indonesian women appear to approve of male headship while only 44% of Pakistani women approve. Indonesian approval of patriarchy is reinforced by the marriage law, which institutionalizes male headship, and the common view of students that women should be 'secondary earners' (Utomo 2012). In contrast, much higher percentages of Indonesians have very 'modern' views of women's role in society and approve of women participating in all areas of public life.

A possible explanation of this puzzling anomaly is that 'patriarchy' is experienced as more 'benign' in Indonesia than it is in Pakistan. In Pakistan, women experience more restrictions on their participation in public life, education and advancement. For example, educational levels of women in Pakistan are much lower than those of men, whereas in Indonesia they are almost equal. Indonesian women do not feel as oppressed by male leadership in the family because they wield many kinds of power in society. The head of the MUI in Batu Sangkar explained that, in the home, the man is the head of the family, but in public life men and women are equal. Women can be top leaders over men in politics, business, education and all other fields.

'Patriarchy' is a one dimensional oversimplification when it comes to a complex society like Indonesia. 'Heterarchy' may hint at more of the complexity. Crumley (1995, 3) defines heterarchy as 'the relation of elements to one another when they are unranked or when they possess the potential for being ranked in a number of different ways'. Heterarchy does not deny the reality of patriarchy in some dimensions of life, but patriarchy is not the only form of social organization. In some dimensions of life, there may be matriarchy or no particular hierarchy. In Indonesia, public and private spaces are not as divided from each other as in Western societies. It is not unusual in Indonesia to meet a woman who is an activist for gender equality, but imagines her husband as the head of the family. She imagines herself as the mother (*ibu*) of her household, who manages her husband, children, servants and finances, all the while teaching full-time and earning the bulk of the household income.

The complexity of Indonesian social imaginaries about women is illustrated by the phenomenal popularity of the current Minister of Oceans and Marine Resources, Susi Pujiastuti. Pujiastuti breaks all of the stereotypes of a good, Javanese, Muslim woman. She is widely perceived as effective, hard-working, honest, courageous, frank and tough. The press revels in showing shocking pictures of her smoking, riding a man's motorcycle with no helmet, revealing a tattoo, stretching her legs while blowing up illegal fishing boats, telling jokes about taboo topics like corruption, etc. Pujiastuti dropped out of high school because of political activism and went on to become a highly successful business woman. She is also twice divorced and a single mother. Pujiastuti deconstructs traditional images of a 'good Muslim woman' and expands the Indonesian social imaginary of a national hero.

Pujiastuti's popularity may be facilitated by an imaginary of women as equal to men in the public sphere, especially where their role does not interfere with the imaginary of men as leaders in the home and in the sphere of religion. According to Reid (2014b), for many centuries Indonesia (and Southeast Asia generally) enjoyed a far greater balance between the roles of men and women in the public sphere than Europe or the Middle East, especially before the acceptance of Western patriarchal modernity at the height of the Victorian era. That this imaginary still has power in contemporary Indonesia is revealed in the comment by the head of the MUI in West Sumatra, that subordination of women to men only applies in the home, not in the public sphere. When the Islamic Sultanate of Aceh appointed four sultanas in a row in the seventeenth century, one reason may have been that sultanas, as women, would not interfere with the intense theological conflict between ulamas about Islamic mysticism (Reid 2014b). Today, Muslim feminists are beginning to gently challenge male dominance, even in the sphere of religion, facilitated by the emergence of women with doctorates in Islamic studies.[13]

## 5. Conclusion

*Adat* traditional law, Islamic law and national law are construed in Indonesia as complementary to each other. There is one Supreme Court, which has jurisdiction over all. Nevertheless, there are often tensions or even contradictions between different sources. The resolution of these tensions is not achieved by applying a hierarchy of universal legal principles, but rather through a discourse that tries to find the most appropriate solution to human problems in a particular time and place. The bad news is that this 'flexible' view of law means that women cannot just appeal to the Constitution or to international human rights conventions that have been legally ratified by Indonesia. National law often has less authority than traditional *adat* or religious law. On the other hand, the good news is that the same applies to Islamic law (*fiqh*). Most Indonesians do not regard Islamic law as universal, absolute and inviolable, but rather as a discursive tradition, subject to varying viewpoints and interpretations.

Sometimes, tradition and religion seem to conspire together (and against national law), to hold women in a position of subordination to patriarchal structures. However, women are traditionally powerful in many Indonesian ethnic groups. Today, 99.4% of young Indonesian women are literate. The phenomenal growth of education among Indonesian women has led to more and more women taking top leadership positions in politics, education and religion. Both law and social structures seem to lag behind the experience of Indonesian women as powerful subjects who share in constructing the future of Islamic civilization in Indonesia and beyond.

## Notes

1. This case study, presented here in a highly compressed and simplified version, is taken from Bowen (2003, 35–43).
2. Interview with the author during a workshop at the Faculty of Cultural Sciences, Universitas Andalas, Padang, West Sumatra (Minangkabau) on 31 July 2015.
3. Interview with Ulama Wannofri Samry, Head of MUI, at his home in Batu Sangkar on 1 August 2015.
4. Women often work in the 'informal sector', running food stalls, catering, trading in the marketplace, selling snacks or providing services such as laundry to the many students who live in the area. Informal sector businesses are not registered or licensed, do not pay taxes and are not recorded in the GNP. They usually operate with a tiny profit margin and may be subject to extortion by local gangsters (*preman*).
5. *Kejawen* is often translated as 'Javanese mysticism'. It is a complex mixture of supernatural beliefs and practices handed down from the ancestors.
6. See http://www.gallup.com/poll/142727/religiosity-highest-world-poorest-nations.aspx. Accessed 5 March 2016.
7. Most Indonesian Muslims are Sunnis who are strongly influenced by the Shāfi'ī school (*mazhab*) of jurisprudence. However, Muhammadiyah (with 20–30 million members) is considered 'non-*mazhab*' and emphasizes independent judgement (*ijtihad*).
8. According to a survey carried out by the Center for Population Studies at Universitas Gadjah Mada, Yogyakarta. See http://cpps.ugm.ac.id/pages/penelitian. Accessed 5 March 2016.

9. The following 14 points were enumerated by the committee led by Siti Masdah Mulia as problematic for women who are concerned with human rights. Mulia and her colleagues addressed these points in the CLD (see Mulia 2008). Note that these 14 points are only a small part of the CIL. There are many wise and admirable points in the CIL, which are not commented on here.

10. Legislation is currently under consideration that would raise the minimum marital age for women to make it the same as for men.

11. Aceh, in the extreme North of Sumatra, is the only province in Indonesia that has special permission to apply *Syari'a* law within the province. Certain counties within some other provinces have passed local laws (*perda*) based on *Syari'a*. However, they are subject to legal challenge if they violate constitutional rights. Recently, local *Syari'a* legislation has not proved popular and in some cases has been withdrawn.

12. This figure is based on an informal (non-scientific) survey in the middle of Islamabad at midday. I stood on a busy corner and counted all the men and women who passed by for one hour: 90% were men.

13. See Syamsiyatun in Adeney-Risakotta (2014).

## Disclosure statement

No potential conflict of interest was reported by the author.

## References

Adeney, Bernard. 1995. *Strange Virtues: Ethics in a Multicultural World*. Downers Grove, IL: InterVarsity Press.

Adeney-Risakotta, Bernard, ed. 2014. *Dealing with Diversity: Religion, Globalization, Violence, Gender and Disasters in Indonesia*. Geneva: Globethics.

Adeney-Risakotta, Bernard. Forthcoming. "Religion, Women and Public Policy: Modern Social Imaginaries about Women in Indonesia." In *Religion, Public Policy and Social Transformation in Southeast Asia, Vol. 2, Gender and Identity*, edited by Dicky Sofjan. Geneva: Globethics.

Adeney-Risakotta, Farsijana. 2005. *Politics, Ritual and Identity in Indonesia: A Moluccan History of Religions and Social Conflict*. Njimegen: The Radboud University. Accessed April 28, 2016. http://webdoc.ubn.ru.nl/mono/r/risakotta_f/poliriani.pdf

Bowen, John R. 2003. *Islam, Law and Equality in Indonesia: An Anthropology of Public Reasoning*. Cambridge: Cambridge University Press.

Crumley, Carole L. 1995. "Heterarchy and the Analysis of Complex Societies." *Archeological Papers of the American Anthropological Association* 6 (1): 1–5.

Doorn-Harder, Pieternella van. 2006. *Women Shaping Islam: Reading the Qur'an in Indonesia*. Champaign: University of Illinois Press.

Geertz, Hildred. 1961. *The Javanese Family: A Study of Kinship and Socialization*. Long Grove, IL: Waveland Press.

Hassan, Riaz. 2002. *Faithlines: Muslim Conceptions of Islam and Society*. Oxford: Oxford University Press.

Hooker, M. B. 2003. *Indonesian Islam: Social Change through Contemporary Fatawa*. Honolulu: University of Hawai'i Press.

Magnis-Suseno, Franz. 1984. *Etika Jawa*. Jakarta: Gramedia.

Mukhotib, ed. 2002. *Menolak Mut'ah dan Sirri: Memberdayakan Perempuan*. Yogyakarta: Yayasan Kesejahteraan Fatayat.

Mulia, Siti Musdah. 2007. "Toward a Just Marriage Law: Empowering Indonesian Women through a Counter Legal Draft to the Indonesian Compilation of Islamic Law." In *Islamic Law in Contemporary Indonesia: Ideas and Institutions*, edited by R. Michael Feener and Mark E. Cammack, 128–145. Cambridge, MA: Harvard University Press.

Mulia, Siti Musdah. 2008. "Menuju Hukum Perkawinan Yang Adil: Memberdayakan Perempuan Indonesia?" In *Perempuan dan Hukum: Menuju Hukum yang Berperspektif Kesetaraan dan Keadilan*, 2nd ed., edited by Sulistyowati Irianto, 144–172. Jakarta: Yayasan Obor Indonesia.

Naipaul, V. S. 1998. *Beyond Belief: Islamic Excursions among the Converted Peoples*. London: Vintage, Random House.

Nurmila, Nina. 2008. "Negotiating Polygamy in Indonesia: Between Islamic Discourse and Women's Lived Experiences." In *Indonesian Islam in a New Era: How Women Negotiate Their Muslim Identities*, edited by Susan Blackburn, Bianca J. Smith, and Siti Syamsiyatun, 23–46. Melbourne: Monash University Press.

Rachmah, Ida. 2008. "Muslim Women and Contemporary Veiling in Indonesian Sinetron." In *Indonesian Islam in a New Era: How Women Negotiate Their Muslim Identities*, edited by Susan Blackburn, Bianca J. Smith, and Siti Syamsiyatun, 47–68. Clayton: Monash University Press.

Reid, Anthony. 2014a. *Patriarchy and Puritanism in Southeast Asian Modernity*. DORISIA Working Paper 8. http://www.dorisea.de/sites/default/files/DORISEA%20WP%208%20Reid%20Patriarchy%20and%20Puritanism%20in%20Southeast%20Asian%20Modernity.pdf

Reid, Anthony. 2014b. "Urban Respectability and the Maleness of (Southeast) Asian Modernity." *Asian Review of World Histories* 2 (2): 147–167.

Ricklefs, M. C. 2012. *Islamisation and Its Opponents in Java c. 1930 to the Present*. Honolulu: University of Hawai'i Press.

Smith, Bianca J. 2008. "Kejawen Islam as Gendered Praxis in Javanese Village Religiosity." In *Indonesian Islam in a New Era: How Women Negotiate Their Muslim Identities*, edited by Susan Blackburn, Bianca J. Smith, and Siti Syamsiyatun, 97–118. Clayton: Monash University Press.

Utomo, A. J. 2012. "Women as Secondary Earners: Gendered Preferences on Marriage and Employment of University Students in Modern Indonesia." *Asian Population Studies* 8 (1): 65–85.

# Between Texts and Contexts: Contemporary Muslim Gender Roles

Shamim Samani

**ABSTRACT**

Based on research conducted in Western Australia as part of a PhD thesis, this article looks at the shifting boundaries of gender roles in Australian Muslim households. It highlights the Islamic stance on the biological differences between men and women as the basis for understanding gender roles and responsibilities. It also uncovers how the ideal influences contemporary Muslim gender roles and the interplay of social and economic factors that impact upon Australian Muslim households in their acculturation in the more liberal Western setting. In order to capture the nuances of perceptions and accounts of how the participants in the research perceive providing and caring roles in the household unit, the primary research uses narrative enquiry as part of its methodology. The findings show that there is variance between the textual injunctions and contextual realties as Muslim women also become providers for the household. While this shows that there is congruence with the mainstream Australian society, it also has implications for how gender equality and economic empowerment of women are approached in a diverse society like Australia.

## Introduction

The move for gender equality globally has called for a reconstruction of gender roles to suit a more equitable division of labour within households and increased opportunities for women in the public sphere. As a universal standard, it provides the basis for discussion on the position and status of women and concerted international progress towards this can be observed in the work of the United Nations Commission on the Status of Women (UN Women 2014). The momentum for gender equality in Australia, increasing over time, reflects the trends seen in many Western countries with a focus on economic security and women's participation in the public space. While the approach to attaining equality is based on 'shared' experiences of women, reports (for example, the Gender Equality Blueprint [AHRC 2010]) recognize that demographic factors such as ethnicity, age and socio-economic status play a role in advancing women's progress in these areas. Largely subsumed in differences related to cultural and linguistic diversities, what appear to be missing in the national discourse are the differences in the ways gender roles are perceived and acted upon. Little attention is paid to how non-secular groups view gender relations, and how this influences the household division of labour and women's economic roles. In opening up this debate to include faith groups as part of the discussion on gender equality and gender roles, this article, which is based on research conducted at Curtin University in Western Australia, contributes to the discourse by examining the nuances of Muslim gender roles through both theological and social lenses.

## Sociological and religious approaches to gender relations

The major difference between sociological and religious approaches to gender is found around the notion of creation or social construction and consequently the roles men and women play in the household unit as providers and carers (Smith 1987; Storkey 2001; Holmes 2007). Drawing on biological determination and social constructs, Holmes (2007) for example, differentiates between sex as an evolutionary difference and gender as a product of cultural and social processes. Similarly, Wright and Rogers (2010) argue that, while women in all societies have historically had responsibility for early childcare, these responsibilities have been modified by specific economic, political and cultural contexts such as a move away from agrarian economies, urbanization and technological advances. In contemporary times, social and legal modifications have played a role in improving gender equity and increasing opportunities for women outside the domestic space, even in Muslim majority countries (see Offenhauer 2005; Rashad, Osman, and Roudi-Fahimi 2005 for more).

   Gender roles viewed from an Islamic perspective are based on the qur'anic account of creation, which states that the first human being to be created was Adam and that his partner, Hawwa (Eve) was created from him, and from their offspring other human beings spread over the earth. The Islamic scholar, Maududi (2000, 305–306), for example, discusses this not only in the context of obligations towards other human beings but also in relation to family and kinship. In his commentary, Maududi touches on the observance of family ties and kinship obligations. This perspective stresses the importance of the family, with clearly defined household roles for men and women on which to build society. As a building block for society, the family is accentuated in Islahi's (2001, 117) statement that '... a stable and well-organised family system is a prerequisite for the birth of a righteous society'. This model is based on explicit injunctions in the Qur'an (that imply gender role expectations) and the teachings of the early Muslim jurists. Roald (2001, 145) observes that the model has attained a 'sacrosanct' position in Muslim societies. Religious scholars such as Doi (2005), Islahi (2001) and Badawi (1995) stress the importance of kinship ties within an extended family system and the family institution, with men as providers and household heads, and women as care-givers. In return for care-giving, the financial rights of women are endorsed through the entitlement to *nafaqa*, which includes 'feeding, clothing, shelter, medication and general care' (Aliyu 2010, 45), even when a women may be wealthier than her husband. Doi (2005, 106) explains that the maintenance is *wājib* (obligatory) and Mir Husseini (2007, 8) details that, while the husband is the sole owner of matrimonial resources, a wife is entitled to whatever she brings into the marriage and any earnings during the marriage. Siddiqi (1988, 71) states that, if a husband refuses to provide economic sustenance to his wife, there are grounds for dissolving the marriage through a Muslim family court. Most Muslim majority countries have what Rahim (2011, 1) calls 'quasi-secular' systems in which established Islamic family codes are incorporated in the legal system, and Muslim courts can rule on family disputes. Rahim (2011, 2) explains that these are a legacy of the post-colonial, secular-oriented constitutional and political frameworks adopted by many Muslim majority states. For instance, even though the Egyptian Constitution has its roots in English common law, according to Egyptian family law, a husband's support covers food, clothing, housing, medical treatment and 'such expenses as considered necessary pursuant in Islamic law' (Dahl 1997, 147). Some non-Muslim majority countries in Asia and Africa, such as India, Singapore, Kenya and Uganda, also recognize a parallel Islamic family code for arbitration in Muslim personal cases on matters regarding marriage, divorce, maintenance and custody of children. Anecdotal and other evidence shows that in Australia, too, in the absence of any religious legal recourse for personal issues, matters are resolved through the mediation of sheikhs (religious leaders) in cases of family disputes. The challenges of navigating the two systems – religious and secular – were highlighted in an ABS Television documentary called 'Divorce: Aussie Islamic Way' (ABC 2011). It followed a number of Muslim couples and sheikhs seeking to resolve marital disputes and divorce issues. The insights provided are captured in the producer's comment:

> There is a perception that Islamic religious practice is set in stone, but it is not the case. Divorce: Aussie Islamic Way shows that Islamic law is subject to different interpretations and that qualified sheikhs take into account social circumstances and social values when they apply Islamic law. (O'Hara 2011)

While gender roles are clearly specified in ideals, contemporary Muslim households show a move away from the extended family and male-headed households to nuclear units (Ashrafi 1992; Hoodfar 1997; Roy 2004; Offenhauer 2005). Offenhauer (2005, 2) points out that ' ... In many Muslim states, the substance of family law and its actual implementation differ in ways that somewhat mitigate the gender imbalance of laws on the books'. Attitudes towards women's economic participation are also changing and women increasingly share in the role of providing for the family unit. This is evidenced both in the West and in Muslim majority societies. Muslims in the West are largely migrants and households comprise immediate family members only. Contributions by both men and women are often important for family finances. Consistent women's labour force participation with parenting interruptions is also seen within Muslim families. Inglehart and Pippa (2009, 4) find that Muslim migrant populations, even though primarily socialized in the religious cultures of their countries of origin, are continually adapting to Western lifestyles. This is also evidenced in Australia.

## Research overview

Although the Muslim presence in Australia dates back to the seventeenth century, it was not until after World War II that a significant household and communal presence was noticeable. The majority of the early cameleers from Afghanistan and northern India who helped to open up the interior returned home after short contracts (Uniya 2003). It was not until the 1970s that a significant community presence was seen, with Muslims from Albania, Bosnia, Turkey and Lebanon settling in Australia. Since the beginning of the twenty-first century, Muslims have come from diverse countries including Malaysia, Indonesia, Iraq, Iran, Fiji, Egypt, India, Somalia and Pakistan. According to the 2011 census, 61.5% of Muslims in Australia had been born overseas (ABS 2012). Earlier estimates show that approximately 28% were born in the

Middle East or North Africa, 16% in Asia; 9% in Europe, 4% in Africa (excluding North Africa) and 3% in Oceania (excluding Australia) (HREOC 2004, 213). Consequently, many Muslim women are first-generation Australian, but a large number were born in Australia and the families of some converts to Islam have been in Australia for three or more generations. This article therefore examines gender roles in light of the influence of countries of origin and adaptation to Australian society.

The findings in this article are based on research conducted in Perth, Western Australia, completed in 2010. As part of the study, 20 Muslim women from metropolitan Perth were interviewed to investigate how they perceive gender relations and what factors have a bearing on contemporary Muslim gender roles in Australia. The participants were Sunni Muslim women. Sunni Islam is followed by about 87–90% of Muslims worldwide (Pew Research Centre 2009) and accounts for the majority of the Muslim population in Australia (Saeed 2003). Though Shia Muslims share the same religious foundations, aspects of their texts and practices differ markedly from the Sunni belief system. The focus on Sunni Muslim women provided some consistency in religious cultural backgrounds, and the specific context for the study.

A qualitative approach using narrative enquiry was used as the research method. Clandinin and Rosiek (2007) explain that, while a narrative may be oral or written and produced through fieldwork, an interview or a conversation, narrative enquiry is in essence the study of accounts that explain human experience. It focuses on the meanings that people ascribe to their experiences. A purposive recruitment strategy was used and the participants were recruited through personal contacts, contacts within various Muslim welfare organizations, and Muslim social networks. All the participants identified themselves as Muslims. The depth in the narratives of the participants was not geared to compute collective values for application from a sample to the Muslim community as a whole. Rather, the design of the research was to open up new meanings for understanding the patterning of gender relations and roles through the perspectives of the participant women.

This research has a number of limitations. Foremost, due to resource constraints, it was focused on the views of only Muslim women. A more holistic representation would have been obtained if it had extended to include the perspectives of Muslim men, too. Further, as a stand-alone study, it did not allow for comparisons with other faith groups, who may also view gender relations and roles from a theological perspective. And finally, the sample group did not differentiate between levels of practice of Islam, although more conservative Muslims may view gender relations and roles differently from less conformist groups or individuals.

The participants were born in 10 different countries: Australia, Afghanistan, Bangladesh, Egypt, Eritrea, Indonesia, Malaysia, Singapore, Somalia and South Africa. Most of the women were first-generation Australians, having come to Australia as migrants with their families. Three were second-generation Australians, born in Australia, both with parents born outside Australia. Two women were of Anglo-Celtic background – one a third-generation Australian, and the other a fifth-generation Australian; were both converts to Islam. The majority of the women were between 20 and 30 years old. With regard to their marital status, 13 were married, six were single and one was divorced. Their household sizes ranged from one to five members of the immediate family. The single women lived with their families and the divorced woman on her own.

Although the sample design did not actively seek tertiary educated women, in terms of education, 10 of the participants had completed a Bachelor's degree. Three were enrolled in a Bachelor's programme and one in a doctoral programme, and one had deferred study. Unable to find employment in her field, one woman with a PhD had decided to enrol in a diploma programme to enhance her employment prospects. Two were medical doctors; one was an intern at a local hospital in Perth, while the other, unable to have her qualifications recognized in Australia, had reskilled through various short courses. The rest of the women had achieved tertiary qualifications or the equivalent of Year 12. Cook (2011, 1) finds that compared with the Australian population as a whole, the Muslim population in Australia has higher educational attainment, both at the tertiary and secondary levels. Cook (2011, 1) finds that Muslims are more likely to than the Australian population as a whole to have the equivalent of Year 12 education. Her analysis of the 2006 census showed that 18.5% of Muslims had a Bachelor's degree, compared with 15.6% of the general population.

All of the women indicated that they had received some form of Islamic education, in either formal or informal settings. One had completed studies at an Islamic seminary overseas and two young women had been educated in integrated curriculum schools at both primary and secondary levels. Muslim communities in Australia have established a number of schools that offer the public school curriculum together with Islamic religious education (see Clyne 2003, for more). The two convert participants had an understanding of Islam through reading and through attending various forums for Islamic education. See Table 1 for demographic details of the sample group.

## Diversities in Muslim gender relations

The narratives showed how the intersectionalities between religious orientation, regional developmental patterns and migration affect the way gender roles are perceived.

The underlying theme that emerged in the narratives was that the household organization and roles within it are modeled on the guidelines in Islam. The fundamental

**Table 1.** Selected demographics.

| Age | No. of participants | Marital status | No. of participants | Work type | No. of participants |
|---|---|---|---|---|---|
| 20–30 | 8 | Married | 13 | Full time | 6 |
| 30–40 | 3 | Single | 6 | Part time or casual | 12 |
| 40–50 | 5 | Divorced | 1 | Volunteer | 2 |
| 50+ | 4 | | | | |

| Countries of birth | No. of participants | Level of education | No. of participants | No. of children | No. of participants |
|---|---|---|---|---|---|
| Afghanistan | 1 | PhD completed | 1 | 0 | 6 |
| Australia | 5 | PhD enrolled | 1 | 1 | 5 |
| Bangladesh | 2 | Bachelors completed | 10 | 2 | 3 |
| Egypt | 1 | Bachelors enrolled | 3 | 3 | 2 |
| Eritrea | 1 | Bachelors deferred | 1 | 4 | 1 |
| Indonesia | 1 | Tertiary or Year 12 completed | 4 | 5 | 3 |
| Malaysia | 3 | | | | |
| Singapore | 2 | | | | |
| Somalia | 2 | | | | |
| South Africa | 2 | | | | |

importance of the family institution as the 'crux of everything' (Interviewee 013, age: 40–50) ran strongly in the narratives. The narratives pointed out that the responsibilities of both parents were crucial to the family's well-being. There was a general impression of the husband as household head, but the participants also pointed out that men and women had shared responsibility for the welfare of their families. In comparing with the mainstream, some women perceived that the fundamentals of family life were similar and that the core values of Muslim households were similar to those of non-Muslim Australians: 'I also don't think there is much difference in the mainstream Anglo-Celtic families in gender relations – the man is still the household head in those relationships' (Interviewee 005, age: 50–60). The major perceived difference was that men are sanctioned as head of the family within Islam.

This sanction is observed in the concept of *qiwāma* (commonly translated as guardianship), which is stressed in Q 4.34. Maududi (2000, 333) explains that the Arabic term 'stands for a person who is responsible for the right conduct, safeguard and maintenance of the affairs of an individual, an institution or an organisation. Thus, man is the governor, director, protector and manager of the affairs of women'. The verse is generally interpreted as bestowing on men the responsibility to provide for their families and as conferring a leadership role. There are several interpretations of the term *qiwāma*, and Muslim feminist scholarship challenges the view that it gives superiority to men (see for instance Mernissi 1987; Wadud-Mushin 1992; Al-Hibri 2000; Barlas 2002). The duty of guardianship can be translated as giving men the superior role of decision maker within the household and provides the basis for establishing a hierarchy within the marital relationship. According to Roald (2001), some interpretations of the term contain authoritarian elements, but others mention the quality of benevolence. The role of guardian (*qawāma*) emerged in the narrative of one young women, who felt the need to get married in order to have a male guardian when she was close to finishing secondary school, but decided against it for two reasons: first, because she wanted to pursue higher education and, second, because she felt that being Australian born and bred, she was not bound by any cultural expectations and did not need a guardian to accomplish anything:

> I would think that, I should get married. It would be easier being a Muslim. You need to have that protection in the form of a male, having a male with you always, but then I thought it would not be the right thing to do because I want to do [further studies] … I do not have any of these boundaries. (Interviewee 002, age: 20–30)

Such protection underlies the restrictions imposed on women in countries where Islamic Sharia law prevails, such as Saudi Arabia, where women are restricted from travelling without a *maḥram* (permitted male escort). A human rights report (Erturk 2009, 10) found that, while there have been reforms and positive developments in women's access to education, Saudi Arabia remains a sex-segregated society in which there are limits to women's autonomy, freedom of movement and employment because they are legally under male guardianship. More recent female activism against the authority of male guardianship and the rights of women has resulted in further reforms including the right of women to vote (Al Jazeera 2014, 2015).

Other narratives showed relatively similar attitudes to role expectations. Bouma, Daw, and Munawar (2001) find that, since there are varying degrees of cultural and religious diversity, there are no common patterns in adaptation to the Australian cultural milieu across Muslim communities. However, there are patterns related to countries of origin. Comparing cultural patterns, the young participant mentioned above, observed a trend towards finishing high school:

> A lot of people that I knew from one section of the community [*mostly Middle Eastern*] were all getting married and I thought that was the thing to do. It is the kind of thing to do when you are more cultural, traditional and all that, but then when I went to uni [I saw] that it is different in Malaysia, girls study and then get married, that there are women who are 30 and not married yet. (Interviewee 002, age: 20–30)

The participant went on to share that these expectations were probably suitable for women who had been socialized within that cultural pattern but would not suit someone like herself. Rashad, Osman, and Roudi-Fahimi (2005, 2) note that marriage in Middle Eastern cultures, where the status of women is mainly defined by their roles as wives and mothers, is a 'turning point that bestows prestige, recognition and societal approval on both partners, particularly the bride'. However, they also point out regional diversities, such that women from countries such as Egypt, Jordan, Lebanon and Palestine have an educational gap in their favour and are delaying marriage.

The historical developmental trajectory of Middle Eastern cultures was highlighted in the narrative of a participant from Egypt:

> My mother is 65 and she is the one that got the scholarship to go to America, not my dad. And that was in 1974, … If you look at Egypt from 1970 there were so many women that were educated, that were learning, that had high degrees … (Interviewee 008, age: 30–40)

Egypt has an early and sustained history of modernization, female participation in the public sphere and strong female activism. The country's 1962 Charter stated that 'Woman must be regarded as equal to man and must therefore shed the remaining shackles so that she might take a constructive and profound part in shaping life' (Badran 1991, 218). State-implemented policies focused on women have, on the one hand, aided nation-building in many parts of the Muslim world, and at the same time they have resulted in shifts in household gender dynamics. This was also reflected in the comments of a participant originally from Bangladesh:

> My mother was a doctor and my father was also working, but my mother was working more than him. My mother was doing three jobs and my father basically gave all the money to my mother. This is in Bangladesh! (Interviewee 003, age: 40–50).

This can be explained through strategic interventions as part of the broader paradigm of women and development (through aid-dependency in the case of Bangladesh), which have enabled a large number of women to be educated and participate in the public sphere (Kabeer 1994, 126).

Similar regional differences were noted in the comments of another participant, whose parents were also from Bangladesh:

> There is a stereotyping that the man is the household head. Like my mum has more say than my dad … They both work and study, that is the way society is now; both parents work, do the housework, different proportions in different families … (Interviewee 020, age: 20–30)

As noted previously, these narratives suggest regional differences in expected gender roles related to the socio-cultural regions that the women come from, which are influenced by development policies across generations.

Other inter-generational differences in gender relations and roles followed a more traditional pattern when the participants shared that they saw distinct roles in their parents' relationships, with mothers as homemakers and fathers as providers. In comparison, they saw their own relationships patterned as more egalitarian, with both spouses working and sharing in household chores. A young participant of Eritrean heritage, commented:

> It is totally different from my relationship with my husband. I don't think my dad would get up and cook or do something. My mum would probably be the housekeeper and the cook and everything. My dad would be the breadwinner. It is very different from the way we are; even the way we communicate ... (Interviewee 010, age: 20–30)

A similar inter-generational difference was also disclosed by a young participant originally from Indonesia. Although her mother was educated, she had prioritized looking after the family over earning an extra income: 'My mum has always been a stay-at-home mum, but in terms of her education she has an equivalent of Master's degrees in Arabic and Islamic studies' (Interviewee 001; age: 20–30). This indicates that some Muslim women may choose to prioritize caring over career-building.

The process of socialization in particular gender roles emerged in the words of a young woman from South Africa. She shared that many older Muslim South African women are highly active in the public social and economic spheres, but other ethnic groups may have been socialized as primary household care-givers and it would be difficult to shift such perceptions: 'This is how they have been conditioned; what they believe in and you are now telling them that it's not the way it is' (Interviewee 015, age: 20–30). This indicates that Muslim migrant women may not necessarily see their roles changing in the process of migration. When men are able to provide for families, women may continue to choose or be obliged to remain in primary caring roles.

While these features characterize some of the household patterns seen in Australian Muslim households, an interesting observation was made by one of the convert participants. She shared an appreciation of the distinct roles for men and women in the household, which provide her with a 'framework' to work with:

> After converting, I slowly learnt that there were distinctive roles men and women would need to play and learnt to appreciate that value more – (*You value that more?*) – exactly! When I was younger, having that freedom, it was very confusing because at the end, females are built differently to males. Yes, men cannot have children – physiological differences ... With Islam as I have come to learn and appreciate, Islam enables it, it says: it's okay. The highest priority is to be the parents, you know, be the housewife and that's a very valuable role ... (Interviewee 018, age: 30–40).

The physiological differences mentioned here are the basis of much of the line of reasoning within Islamic texts regarding the characterization of gender roles as carers and guardians. Shafaat (1984), for instance, sees two reasons for men being given the role of guardian: first, that men are stronger than women and have the physical ability to protect women and, second, that men spend out of their means (due to the imposition of the duty of economic responsibility). At the same time, according to him, the role of protection goes beyond economic and physical protection, extending to supporting the psychological and emotional needs of women.

The value of an Islamic model on which to moderate gender roles and responsibilities also emerged in the comments of the divorced participant, who felt that she could have done more to save her marriage by adhering to prescribed roles:

> We didn't take it seriously … , I certainly didn't, only just from what I know and heard, not gone out to search and learn about it and get an *imam* to talk to my husband to myself … Definitely having a model on which to base your relationship would have helped. (Interviewee 016, age: 50–60)

Here, the participant refers to learning more about the regulations on gender relations from a religious leader. As mentioned previously, since there is no regulatory body on Muslim family law in Australia, family disputes are often referred to religious leaders to mediate or resolve.

## Economic and social challenges

While most Muslims still accept the principles based on the qur'anic account of creation, simplistic interpretations are not workable as many Muslim women find themselves playing different roles in the public sphere. Most participants highlighted the challenge of economic imperatives impacting upon the way gender relations are patterned: 'Modern lifestyle applies increasing pressures to have two incomes, more opportunities to develop, study, so there has to be a compromise of traditional roles' (Interviewee 015, age: 20–30); 'It goes without saying that it is among Muslims and non-Muslims – like the two incomes, no kids lifestyle' (Interviewee 002, age: 20–30); 'You need the double income to survive and you have a mortgage and this and this and this to pay so I think things have changed a lot' (Interviewee 007, age: 20–30). As these narratives show, many Muslims aspire to modern lifestyles that require a high level of income to maintain a good standard of living. A report by the National Centre for Economic Modelling (Phillips, Jinjing, and Matthew 2012) finds that cost of living pressures are fuelled by rises in cost over time of essentials such as electricity, rent, mortgages, fuel and public transport. Besides these basic utilities, costs of living are also related to discretionary items to meet the demands of a modern lifestyle.

A significant reflection across the narratives was the pull between cultures when exposure to the liberal and more egalitarian Australian culture leaves some young Muslims confused about their traditional roles. The focus of Islamic discourse is idealistic, ennobling the roles of men as providers and women as household care-givers, yet the practicalities are different. For instance, Zainab al-Ghazzāli's commentary on *qiwāma* (as quoted in Roald 2001, 151) states that

> the wife is the one in charge of the family (*walīyatu amrihi*) within the home. She is responsible towards God for the soundness of her husband and her children … *qiwāma* demands from the man the best treatment and equity (*inṣāf*) concerning her in every matter whereof she is in need of any service. He is responsible for protecting her dignity, her honour, and her humanity …

Though such ideals exist, it is unclear how well they are socialized within individual households. As the narratives reveal, the contexts of social realities are mottled, blending tradition with modernity, and there is a blurring of lines between men and women as providers:

> I have a friend who wishes that her husband would feel that responsibility more; that he would be proud to be the provider. He does work, but does not feel the responsibility, wherein she feels that he should be proud of being the provider. (Interviewee, 001, age: 20–30)

Whereas the ideal teaches male responsibilities to be providers, the liberal Australian lifestyle encourages both partners to be income earners and share in household duties. For many young Muslims, the practical pattern is not one where women remain within the home and men go out to work, and balancing the practical with the ideal can be a struggle.

The pull between a traditional, religious model and that of the more mainstream, liberal Australian one was highlighted as straining the cross-cultural marriage between this Australian convert and her husband, who originates from Pakistan: 'He expects me to assist like in providing an income for the family. He expects that I will take care of anything to do with my daughter … the understanding is that I am the primary caregiver … ' (Interviewee 017, age: 20–30). This was further taken up within the narratives of other young women who questioned the ideal as a reference frame. Even though there are inferences from within the Islamic discourse that they would like to adhere to, some young women shared the ambiguity that lies in applying the Islamic model satisfactorily in contemporary times. One participant, for example, spoke of the complexity of religion, culture of origin and exposure to a Western lifestyle impacting on gender relations:

> You have grown up in the Western world. You feel that you adhere to the Qur'an and the *Sunnah*. It still does not provide you with enough reference because it is like this is what the Qur'an and the *Sunnah* says, but how do you put that within your culture, how do you interpret that it is really … (Interviewee 012, age: 20–30)

Another participant shared similar uncertainty over gender roles:

> It is no longer very clear as to what they are responsible for and a lot of the younger couples that I see this confusion of what is the man's responsibility, what is the female's responsibility is causing tension sometimes and conflict … (Interviewee 007, age: 20–30)

According to this participant, the issue is one of a lack of role models. In countries of origin, the extended family provides various male and female role models. Given the nature of migration of mainly nuclear units, families do not have the extended networks on which to base their gender roles: 'Often they don't have role models to see that as a man this is how I am meant to be acting and this is what I have to do' (Interviewee 007, age: 20–30).

Some Muslim women are themselves skilled migrants who have come to Australia for better economic prospects and studies also show that many Muslim women are acquiring higher education (see Cook 2011) to improve their employment potential. In one case, the participant shared how she experienced a role reversal, in that she was the primary income earner for the family:

> I have got a reversed role. I would say this is the norm of the twenty-first century because women are forward in the economy, in their say and their rights especially in secular Australia … And because I have the earning capacity when my husband can't work I take the role up … (Interviewee 004, age: 40–50)

As in this case, other research by the present author also shows that provision for the family and dependents is a major motivator in Muslim women's participation in the workplace. In addition, changes to the welfare system after the 2006 reforms entail 'mutual obligations' and have led to many income support recipients facing mandatory workforce requirements (Cortis, Cowling, and Meagher 2008). In the Australian welfare context, welfare assistance provided to the unemployed places obligations on the recipient, including: actively seeking work, striving to improve competitiveness in the job market or giving back to the community through volunteering (Yeend 2004). Where previously some Muslim women who received such assistance may have chosen to be stay-at-home mothers, these reforms require them to look for and accept paid work.

By compromising the traditional role of women, the economic benefit acquired through workplace participation can be unsettling within households where women have not previously been income-earners. In the case of women who have not had the opportunity to earn a living in their countries of origin, or who are able to access finances through welfare entitlements in Australia, the financial independence gives them autonomy in spending decisions, as shown in this narrative:

> If you go to work you can be earning money and you can buy … I think it probably does change the [*household*] dynamic. I think it is probably difficult for both husband and wife to start feeling who is the head of the family … I think the man would feel threatened … I do think so because they feel that they are losing the wife or control over the wife. (Interviewee 016, age: 50–60)

Other challenges that emerged were related to the social environment, with pressures on both parents to safeguard family interests. Some women shared that maintaining Islamic values while living within the liberal Australian society was the responsibility of both parents and that they shared this duty with their spouses. Muslim societies maintain and uphold religious values, norms and customs through religious education, mostly by means of the *madrasa* system, which provides the basics of learning to read the Qur'an in Arabic. In Australia, this varies, depending on the availability of learning institutions. Some parents may take their children to such classes on weekends or arrange for an Islamic teacher to teach children at home after school hours. Another option is the integrated curriculum schools, which provide culturally appropriate education that covers both religious and a secular learning. The emphasis in the narratives was that safeguarding family interests was the responsibility of both parents.

## Conclusion

This work finds that contemporary Australian Muslim gender roles do preserve a religious normative based on physiological differences between men and women. However, the normative is also permeated by factors such as financial necessity, socialization in the Australian secular space and taking up opportunities for economic mobility. There is strong evidence of the influence of cultures of countries of origin, as well as of the developmental investments in gender-focused development strategies such as education in countries of origin, which have brought about major transformations in household dynamics, even in Muslim majority countries. The shifting boundaries of gender roles and relations are discernible across generations – the respondents and their parents. In general, there is a move away from traditional cultural set-ups, as households are affected by contemporary economic imperatives and as attitudinal outlooks towards women's contribution to household provision change. Although gender equality in itself can be contested and it is debateable whether these changes actually do work in favour of women, it is clear that there is an erosion of the ideal model in which only men are charged with the duty of being providers and women are seen only as primary care-givers for the family. More in-depth research would provide additional insight into the broader patterns of gender roles and responsibilities in Muslim communities and inform inclusive policies on women's economic security and participation in the public space.

## Disclosure statement

No potential conflict of interest was reported by the author.

## References

(ABC) Australian Broadcasting Corporation. 2011. "Divorce: Aussie Islamic Way." Accessed September 30, 2015. http://www.abc.net.au/tv/guide/abc1/201206/programs/DO0967H001D20 12-06-21T213357.htm

(ABS) Australian Bureau of Statistics. 2012. "Cultural Diversity in Australia: Reflecting a Nation. Stories from the 2011 Census." ABS, June 21. Accessed September 30, 2015. http://www.abs. gov.au/ausstats/abs@.nsf/Lookup/2071.0main + features902012-2013.

(AHRC) Australian Human Rights Commission. 2010. 2010 Gender Equality Blueprint: Everyone, Everywhere, Every Day. Accessed September 30, 2015. https://www.humanrights.gov.au/publications/gender-equality-blueprint-2010.

Al-Hibri, Azizah Yahia. 2000. "Muslim Women's Rights in the Global Village: Challenges and Opportunities." Journal of Law and Religion 15 (1/2): 37–66. Accessed September 30, 2015. http://karamah.org/wp-content/uploads/2011/10/Muslim-Womens-Rights-in-the-Global-Villag e-Challenges-and-Opportunities.pdf.

Aliyu, Ibrahim Ahmad. 2010. Protection of Women's Rights under the Shariah. Kuala Lumpur: Dakwah Corner Bookstore.

Al Jazeera. 2014. "Saudi Women Demand End of Male Control." Al Jazeera, March 2. Accessed October 23, 2015. http://www.aljazeera.com/news/middleeast/2014/03/saudi-activists-demand-end-male-control-201432132928215484.html.

Al Jazeera, 2015. "First Saudi Women Register to Vote." Al Jazeera, August 20. Accessed October 23, 2015. http://www.aljazccra.com/news/2015/06/saudi-women-register-vote-150621081535058.html.

Ashrafi, Talat Ara. 1992. Muslim Women in Changing Perspective. New Delhi: Commonwealth.

Badawi, Jamal. 1995. Gender Equity in Islam: Basic Principles. Indianapolis, IN: American Trust.

Badran, Margot. 1991. "Competing Agenda: Feminists, Islam and the State in Nineteenth- and Twentieth-Century Egypt." In Women, Islam and the State, edited by Deniz Kandiyoti, 201–236. Philadelphia, PA: Temple University Press.

Barlas, Asma. 2002. Believing Women in Islam: Unreading Patriarchal Interpretations of the Qur'an. Austin: University of Texas Press.

Bouma, Gary D, Joan Daw, and Riffat Munawar. 2001. "Muslims Managing Religious Diversity." In Muslim Communities in Australia, edited by Abdullah Saeed and Shahram Akbarzadeh, 53–72. Sydney: University of New South Wales Press.

Clandinin, D. Jean, and Jerry Rosiek. 2007. "Mapping a Landscape of Narrative Inquiry: Borderland Spaces and Tensions." In Handbook of Narrative Inquiry: Mapping a Methodology, edited by D. Jean Clandinin, 35–80. Thousand Oaks, CA: Sage.

Clyne, Irene Donohue. 2003. "Muslim Women: Some Western Fictions." In Muslim Women in the United Kingdom and Beyond: Experiences and Images, edited by Tansin Benn and Haifaa Jawad, 19–38. Leiden: Brill.

Cook, Beth. 2011. "Labour Force Outcomes for Australian Muslims." Paper presented at the 12th Australian Social Policy Conference: Social Policy in a Complex World. Accessed June 16, 2012. http://bsllibrary.org.au/wp-content/uploads/2011/08/Labour-force-outcomes-for-Australian-Muslims.pdf.

Cortis, Natasha, Sarah Cowling, and Gabrielle Meagher. 2008. *Welfare to Work and Vulnerable Parents and Young People in Australia: Lessons from International Experience.* Accessed September 30, 2015. http://www.aracy.org.au/publications-resources/command/download_file/id/164/filename/Welfare_to_work_and_vulnerable_families,_children_and_young_people_in_Australia_-_Lessons_from_international_experience.pdf.

Dahl, Tove Stang. 1997. *The Muslim Family: A Study of Women's Rights.* Translated by Ronald Walford. Oslo: Scandinavian University Press.

Doi, Abdur Rahman. 2005. *Women in Sharia.* Kuala Lumpur: A. S. Noordeen.

Erturk, Yakin. 2009. *Promotion and Protection of all Human Rights, Civil, Political, Economic, Social and Cultural Rights, Including the Right to Development. Report of the Special Rapporteur on Violence against Women, Its Causes and Consequences.* Accessed October 24, 2015. http://www2.ohchr.org/english/bodies/hrcouncil/docs/11session/A.HRC.11.6.pdf.

Holmes, Mary. 2007. *What Is Gender? Sociological Approaches.* Los Angeles, CA: Sage.

Hoodfar, Homa. 1997. *Between Marriage and the Market: Intimate Politics and Survival in Cairo.* Berkley: University of California Press.

(HREOC) Human Rights Equal Opportunities Commission. 2004. *Ismae – Listen: National Consultation on Eliminating Prejudice against Arab and Muslim Australians.* Croydon Park: Human Rights and Equal Opportunities Commission.

Inglehart, Ronald, and Pippa Norris. 2009. "Muslim Integration into Western Cultures: Between Origins and Destinations." HKS Faculty Research Working Paper Series RWP09-007, John F. Kennedy School of Government, Harvard University. Accessed September 30, 2015. http://dash.harvard.edu/bitstream/handle/1/4481625/Norris_MuslimIntegration.pdf?sequence = 1.

Islahi, Muhammad Yusuf. 2001. *Etiquette of Life in Islam.* New Delhi: Markazi Maktaba Islami.

Kabeer, Naila. 1994. *Reversed Realties: Gender Hierarchies in Development Thought.* London: Verso.

Maududi, Sayyid Abul A'la. 2000. *The Meaning of the Qur'an.* Volume 1. Translated by Muhammad Akbar. Lahore: Islamic Publications.

Mernissi, Fatima. 1987. *Beyond the Veil: Male–Female Dynamics in Modern Muslim Society.* Bloomington: Indiana University Press.

Mir Husseini, Ziba. 2007. "Islam and Gender Justice." In *Voices of Islam, vol. 5: Voices of Change,* edited by J. Cornell Vincent and Omid Safi, 85–113. Westport, CT: Praegar.

Offenhauer, Priscilla. 2005. *Women in Islamic Societies: A Selected Review of Social Scientific Literature.* Washington, DC: Federal Research Division, Library of Congress.

O'Hara, Marguerite. 2011. *Divorce Aussie Islamic Way: Muslim Women Caught Between Two Worlds. A Study Guide.* Accessed September 30, 2015. https://abccommercial-production-aws.s3-ap-southeast-2.amazonaws.com/study-guide/assets/Divorce%2520Aussie%2520Islamic%2520Way.pdf.

Pew Research Centre. 2009. *Mapping the Global Muslim Population.* Accessed September 30, 2015. http://www.pewforum.org/2009/10/07/mapping-the-global-muslim-population/.

Phillips, Ben, Li Jinjing, and Taylor Matthew. 2012. "Prices These Days: The Cost of Living in Australia." AMP.NATSEM Income and Wealth Report 31. Accessed September 30, 2015. http://www.natsem.canberra.edu.au/publications/?publication = ampnatsem-income-and-wealth-report-31-prices-these-days-the-cost-of-living-in-australia.

Rahim, Lily Zubaidah. 2011. *Muslims Reclaiming the Democratic Quasi-Secular State.* Accessed September 30, 2015. http://sydney.edu.au/arts/research/rss/downloads/documents/Lily_Rahim_Muslims_%20Reclaiming_the_Quasi-Secular_Democratic_State.pdf.

Rashad, Hoda, Magued Osman, and Farzaneh Roudi-Fahimi. 2005. "Marriage in the Arab World." Population Reference Bureau. Accessed September 30, 2015. http://www.prb.org/pdf05/marriageinarabworld_eng.pdf.

Roald, Anne Sofie. 2001. *Women in Islam: The Western Experience.* London: Routledge.

Roy, Olivier. 2004. *Globalized Islam: The Search for a New Ummah*. London: Hurst.

Saeed, Abdullah. 2003. *Muslims in Australia*. Sydney: Allen & Unwin.

Shafaat, Ahmad. 1984. "A Commentary on the Qur'an 4:34." Accessed September 30, 2015. http://www.themodernreligion.com/women/dv-4-34-shafaat.html.

Siddiqi, Mazheruddin. 1988. *Women in Islam*. New Delhi: Adam Publishers & Distributers.

Smith, Dorothy. 1987. *The Everyday as Problematic: A Feminist Sociology*. Boston, MA: North Western Press.

Storkey, Elaine. 2001. *Created or Constructed: The Great Gender Debate*. Sydney: University of New South Wales Press.

Uniya. 2003. "A Background Brief on Muslims in Australia." Accessed September 30, 2015. http://www.uniya.org/pdf/muslims_lowres.pdf.

UN Women. 2014. "A Brief History of CSW." Accessed September 30, 2015. http://www.unwomen.org/en/csw/brief-history.

Wadud-Mushin, Amina. 1992. *Qur'an and Woman: Rereading the Sacred Text from a Woman's Perspective*. Kuala Lumpur: Fajar Bakti.

Wright, Erik Olin, and Joel Rogers. 2010. *American Society: How It Actually Works*. New York: W. W. Norton & Company.

Yeend, Peter. 2004. "Mutual Obligation/Work for the Dole." E-brief. Parliament of Australia. Accessed October 24, 2015. http://www.aph.gov.au/About_Parliament/Parliamentary_Departments/Parliamentary_Library/Publications_Archive/archive/dole.

# Index